Caroline Cox is Principal Lecturer in Cultural & Historical Studies at the London College of Fashion

GOOD HAIR DAYS

A HISTORY OF BRITISH HAIRSTYLING

CAROLINE COX

Ω

QUARTET BOOKS

First published by Quartet Books Limited in 1999
A member of the Namara Group
27 Goodge Street
London W1P 2LD

A catalogue record for this book is available from the British Library

ISBN 0 7043 8111 7

Text design by Namara
Printed and bound in Great Britain by Creative Print and Design
Wales, Ebbw Vale

To Alex and Lionel

ACKNOWLEDGEMENTS

I would like to thank Sandra Holtby, Elizabeth Rouse, Maggie Norden and the staff at the London College of Fashion library for their support and encouragement.

CONTENTS

Introduction   1

(1) To Dress or to Bob: Hair and Femininity   12

(2) The Hairdresser as Guru   62

(3) From Technological Utopia to Countercultural Attack   132

(4) Towards the Millennium   208

Bibliography   270

Index   272

INT

RO-
DUCTION

**Caroline Cox, 1999
Photograph by
Marc Atkins**

Why do we cut and style our hair? Why has the hairdresser's appointment the potential to be one of the most energizing or traumatic events in life? And what can be worse than having a 'bad hair' day or being accused of sporting a 'pudding bowl' haircut? Such references to hair form part of our daily vocabulary yet hair, unlike dress, which is beginning to recover from its traditional associations with the trivialities of femininity, is rarely subject to serious study. Cutting and styling hair are equally obvious examples of the way we transform the raw into the cooked, thus bringing our bodies into culture, and involve participation in ritualistic and creative behaviour which says much about ourselves.

Throughout history hair has been used to comment, to provide a visual statement helped by the versatility of its make up — it can be curled, shaved, dyed, straightened and greased. It is a prime indicator of gender. Cutting the hair of a baby boy is one of the first rites of passage into a more adult masculinity and its loss an obvious part of the ageing process. As little girls we are initiated into the performance of femininity when mother stops cutting it into the standardized fringe and we enter the portals of the salon for the first time for a style of our own choosing. In the twentieth century, the craft of hairdressing as a professional practice has been dominated by men, yet to sit in a salon and have one's hair styled as opposed to cut is still seen as a female 'thing' and even today women tend to be judged by what's on their head rather than what's in it. To understand this implicit gendering of hair is to note the public reaction to any man who seems overly interested in his own barnet, a prime example being the arts broadcaster Melvyn Bragg.

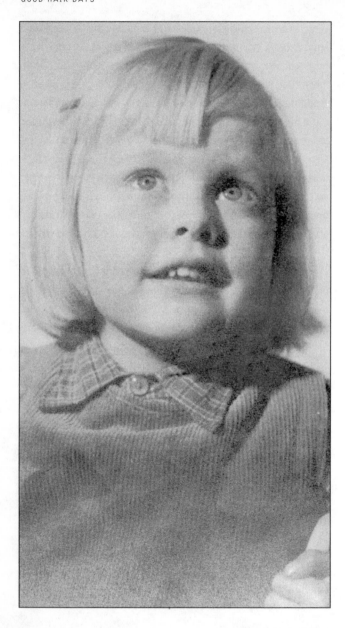

Caroline Cox;
four years old with
'domestic' haircut,
1962

Described by one interviewer as constantly patting and preening his hair as if it was a small pet, the luxuriousness of his locks and his apparent regard for them are viewed suspiciously as self-love, not as something associated with 'real men'. In fact the *Daily Mail* in 1997 ran a whole piece devoted to the changing styles of Bragg's hair from the 'wise old owl look' to the 'hennaed horror'. Likewise the 1970s weave belonging to the television personality Terry Wogan comes in for much criticism. The television critic Victor Lewis-Smith can chart the quintic cycle by which Wogan lives through its various manifestations. Week 1: short back and sides. Week 2: coming on nicely. Week 3: just over the ears. Week 4: getting a bit straggly. Week 5: time to get Week 1 out of the box again.

Hair has such an amazing potential for change that we believe the shaping of it can shift our destinies and a poor haircut can blight the next six months. The hairdresser's appointment thus has magical significance. I can still remember the fear and trepidation on the occasion of my first professional haircut at the salon in the department store of Barlow and Taylor's in Derby. I was not alone in this emotion — most children are terrified, and the education of hairdressers has included the preparation of an infant for this traumatic moment. In 1931 stylists were advised to make sure they did not 'approach any child with a black look or a scowl; with clippers or scissors held glaringly and menacingly in the hand; the very sight of such implements will repulse most children. If the child is nervous, its fears must be allayed. Do not start trying to cut its hair at once, but talk soothingly. Children are plastic little people, and are quite responsive to well-applied kindness and consideration.'[1]

[1] Gilbert Foan, THE ART AND CRAFT OF HAIRDRESSING (London, The New Era Publishing Co. Ltd, 1931), p.140

3

This plastic person was taken to the high street salon as a treat by my grandma at the tender age of six or thereabouts. There my hair was set into curls and I was plonked under a hooded hair-dryer for what seemed a lifetime. My style was then dressed out in front of a mirror while I marvelled at my beetroot red face. I was given a sweet and praised for not howling through the whole ordeal, but after walking around town for a couple of hours the whole lot had gone straight again — still my grandma thought I looked beautiful. From then on important moments in my life like job interviews, weddings, even divorces and funerals called for a new haircut.

The cut is important but these days so is the colour. Myths abound about flaming redheads possessed of a fiery temper and the ubiquitous dumb blonde that reflect the cultural construction of gender, and the personality of the wearer is supposed to be easily deduced from particular cuts and colour. In 1912 Professor R.W. Brown, 'a phrenologist of some repute', lectured regularly on 'How to Tell Character from Hair', enthralling his audiences with analyses of people with light-brown hair who 'invariably manifest a strong predisposition to live more in the province of their sympathies than in the province of their mind' whereas 'the rougher and tougher the hair, the coarser and rougher is the mental and moral nature of the person.' The professor could also predict future employment prospects, believing 'young ladies with red hair excel as waitresses.' In certain curious instances the taxonomy of whole races is interpreted in this way, as in a pseudo-anthropological example of 1935 which found that, 'Dark, almost black, curly hair, found on the heads of many natives of Wales, explains their love of music, singing, their vivacity and enthusiasm, and the "touchy" disposition that is easily pleased

L: Alex Marsden, c. 1980s

R: From a photograph of an insane woman, to show the condition of her hair

[1] Grace A. Rees, READING CHARACTER FROM THE FACE, (London, Right Way Books, 1901) p.72

[2] Charles Darwin, THE EXPRESSION OF THE EMOTIONS, (London, John Murray, 1872), pp.296–7

or offended.'[1] The haircut was also used to indicate some sinister underlying psychiatric disorder by Darwin, who described 'chronic maniacs, who rave incoherently and have destructive impulses,' one having hair that 'rises up from his forehead like the mane of a Shetland pony', and illustrated a woman in whom 'the state of her hair is a sure and convenient criterion of her mental condition'.[2] A 'scientific' picture of the sufferer rather chillingly bears a remarkable resemblance to a photograph of my husband, Alex, taken in the late 1980s. This notion of a hair-style indicating psychological health can be found to a rather less exaggerated extent in an article in *The Globe* which appeared on 16 April 1996 entitled 'Di: Hair Own Story' and purported to chart Princess Diana's state of mind and growing maturity through her changing hair-styles from the '1981 pre-engagement Di' whose 'mousy brown mop suits a shy nursery school assistant' to the hair 'Di-saster' of 1984, which was seen to mirror her 'struggling with Charles and her in-laws'. Her 1996 hair-style was more successful where *après*-divorce she's 'ready to relax with a softer look'. It's amazing she didn't change her hair more dramatically for, as Clairol the dye manufacturers discovered in the 1960s, the most common response amongst women after breaking up was to reach for the bottle and, instead of imbibing gin, become blonde.

Despite this crucial relationship with popular culture the makers of hair-styles suffer from stereotyping and cliché, the camp crimper being one of the most common. This term was said by Vidal Sassoon to have been invented by Edward Morris, a director of the company André Bernard, although its origin is much earlier. When Morris was working in the salon, 'a very haughty lady walked in and demanded, in an eighteen-carat accent, to see Mr Edward. She was speaking to him, of course, but, being a new client, she did not know him. So he said in anxious and appealing tones: "I'm terribly sorry, Madam. He's sick today. But could I be of any service? I'm Fred Crimper." From that moment on we hairdressers had a new label.'[1]

The hairdresser is invariably assumed to be either an insincere flatterer who imposes the latest fashions on duped female consumers, or a rather common sixteen-year-old who asks about holidays in Ibiza with an ear on Radio One. There is also the salon as local gossip shop where old grannies go for therapy, ending up, according to one critic, 'soaking, bedraggled, wrapped in towels like refugees from a shipwreck who find themselves in a cocoon that is comforting, cosy, commonsensical, thick with unmalicious gossip, and the manicurist's recipe for apple crumble, and doggy talk'.[2] Despite being viewed with disdain, the art of hairdressing has a long

[1] Vidal Sassoon, SORRY I KEPT YOU WAITING, MADAM, (London, Cassell and Co. Ltd, 1968), pi

[2] Jonathan Meades, PETER KNOWS WHAT DICK LIKES, (London, Paladin, 1989), p.35

history and is frequently mentioned in literature and depicted in art. This book, however, will focus on the twentieth century, when a pivotal moment within the profession occurs – the division into two types, the ladies' hairdresser and the gentleman's barber. Chapter One deals with the dramatic cultural change from the long dressed hair fashions for women to the bob in the early 1920s. For more than a century a fabulously coiffured wife signified all was well in the male world of work, and quantity rather than quality was what was most admired about a woman's hair. Hairdressing was for the most part undertaken by maids until the early years of the twentieth century, when women began to venture into the salons of the new department stores in most of the major urban centres in Britain. Here false hairpieces fashioned from the hair of working-class women were used to construct intricate styles and so the craft of the posticheur or boardworker was paramount. In opposition men's hair became shorter, taking over from the artistic aesthetic styles of the late nineteenth century which were associated with figures such as Oscar Wilde. At this time venturing into the salon was a hazardous experience as the preparations used in hair care were incredibly dangerous – for instance petrol was in widespread use as an agent for cleaning hair and, when put in close contact with fires used for heating curling tongs, there was an obvious recipe for disaster. Massive changes came in the period immediately before and after the 1914–18 war with the invention in Paris of the bob, which became a widespread fashion in women's hair and led to a decline in elaborate coiffure. Subsequently a boom in ladies' hairdressing occurred, with a concomitant rise in status. With the focus on a changing fashion or aesthetic came the development of the apprenticeship system and hairdressing schools and academies. The introduction of technical literature and a 'scientific' approach to the craft led to the recognition of disorders and diseases in the client and technology began to enter the workplace with machines for hair cutting, singeing, massage, waving and perming. Decorative, dressed hair-styles for women predominated in the nineteenth and early twentieth centuries when long hair was the most insidious symbol of femininity. To have a short haircut was to incite public dismay. Women who sought power and responsibility in society were displayed in the popular press as unwomanly, superfluous and parasitic and tracts such as *Bobbed Hair: Is It Well-pleasing to the Lord?* were distributed, with the irate author interpreting the new fashion as a symbol of moral decline and furiously declaring, 'A "bobbed" woman is a disgraced woman! What will the Lord say to our sisters about this when we all stand at His judgement seat? The refusal to utter the word "obey" in the Marriage Service, the wearing of men's apparel when cycling, the smoking of cigarettes and the "bobbing" of the hair are all indicators of one thing! God's order is everywhere flouted.' This intimates that for men in particular the bob represented more than just a change in hair-style but was symptomatic of deep-rooted changes in society. The bob went on to become one of the first widespread fashions amongst British women in the twentieth century, demonstrating their increasing economic and social independence. It was over forty years before they were prepared to grow their hair long again.

Chapter Two charts the changing social position of the hairdresser from servant to guru, mirroring the couturier's rise within the fashion industry. The profession of hairdresser or coiffeur formed part of the French court in the seventeenth century and they were responsible for creating the highly decorative styles which had evolved amongst the aristocracy as a form of conspicuous consumption, whereas barbers and wigmakers were regarded as mere technicians. As in couture, with the professionalism of the industry came the dominance of men, a situation which still exists today. A liberalism within aristocratic circles meant that women's hair, which had formerly been dressed by other women, was now being cared for by men such as Monsieur Champagne, who worked in the French court from 1635 to the mid-1650s, and as it became more acceptable for a couturier to be a man with female clients (as seen in the career of Charles Frederick Worth in the nineteenth century), so a similar situation occurred in ladies' hairdressing. As the business expanded so the style leaders tended to be male figure-heads and media stars, 'artists' rather than craftsmen — this can be clearly seen in post-war Britain with the publicity given to stars like Mr Teasie Weasie, who held annual shows at the Café de Paris where he introduced new styles like the Champagne Bubble Cut or Boom Line of 1960. Some inroads began to be made by women such as Rose Evansky into the top of the profession, but the hairdresser garnering the most publicity was Vidal Sassoon, whose very definite ideas about styling hair were to be revolutionary. His geometric cuts became symbols of 'Swinging London', leaving women with hair that felt different — instead of being stuck fast with hairspray, it swung.

Chapter Three describes the major techniques developed to change the style, shape and structure of the hair. The perm was one of the most significant technological breakthroughs for hair design in the twentieth century. From its primitive beginnings in the early years of the century, when to have a perm was a somewhat perilous experience, to the developments in chemical perming without the need for machinery, the perm's influence on hair fashions is charted. I remember being intrigued by my grandmother's perm, which never seemed to alter. She sported the same tight curly style in family photographs of the early 1930s right through to the 1990s, which was set at the hairdresser's once a week and permed every six to eight weeks or so. Whenever she came back from the salon she always had a red neck and a slightly flushed face from being under the hooded hair-dryer for a couple of hours, and would be wearing a special net headscarf to protect her new hair-do. It was in the 1930s that women also began to have recourse to the dye bottle in ever increasing numbers, despite the earliest products being notoriously toxic. After several reported cases of rashes and fever through the misuse of paradyes, as they were dubbed, Britain responded with one of the earliest instances of consumer protection in the 1933 Pharmacy and Poison Act, which made warnings on packaging and a patch test a legal requirement in any salon.

The bigger, bolder styles of the 1950s were dependent on all this sort of treatment, together with the availability of new colours and products which created a veritable hair extravaganza until the countercultural styles of the hippie look and its espousal of the natural spelled their demise. Chapter Three also investigates the response by men and women to these changes and the beauty rituals women had to follow at home to spare the expensive upkeep of hard-to-deal-with styles. By the early 1960s the hair-styles promoted by hairdressers created a tension for women between wanting to look fashionable but not wanting to spend most of their lives in the salon. As the 1960s wore on this situation changed dramatically and a revolution in fashion occurred in which hair was to play an important role. Sassoon created easier-to-care-for styles which meant women needed to go to the salon every four to six weeks for a trim as opposed to three times a week to have their plis or sets dressed out. But did all women follow these new functional styles? Not really, and there was a resistance amongst radical feminists, who derided fashion, and working-class women in particular, who equated lots of big hair with a glamorous femininity and were loath to think otherwise. This artificial, sexualized look resurfaced in the 1970s and 1980s, as described in Chapter Four with the emulation of American soap stars, although it seems to have died out in the 1990s, when popular looks are borrowed from sitcom stars such as *Friends*' Jennifer Aniston. There are still strongholds of the style, though, a Jurassic Park of kitsch hair-dos found in American trailer parks, and country and western chanteuses, where it's a significant symbol of survival. Finally, the book discusses the major developments in hair in post-war Britain and traces the key styles and their relationship with culture. As we enter a new millennium the status of the trade has never been so high and hairdressers have the potential to be millionaires, particularly if they are men. Experiments in genetic engineering presage a future where we can decide what colour and texture our children's hair will be from birth. Will the twenty-first century be a time when blondeness is still considered the epitome of femininity or will a new colour lead to the development of a post-millennial construct with a completely different set of meanings of its own?

(1)

TO DRESS BOB: HA AND FEMIN

AND

OR TO

IR
INITY

Long hair, c. 1900s

Throughout European history both men and women have worn very flamboyant hair-styles. During the reign of King Charles I, for instance, there was a popular, rather showy trend amongst aristocratic circles for long, curled and ringleted hair ostentatiously decorated with ribbons and lovelocks, and Louis XIV's wigs reached fantastic heights. By the late nineteenth century, though, decorative hair was regarded as predominantly female and ornate hair-dos, which were once a status symbol for all, began to be linked with women. What had caused this dramatic cultural change, also mirrored in fashionable dress? It's no coincidence that this new hair phenomenon arose at the same time as the increasing disenfranchisement of women, who had no real power in law, were placed squarely within the home and excluded from participation in many aspects of daily life, a result of industrialization and the consequent patterns of social relationships formed by the economic rise of the middle classes. Wives became objects indicating the success of the husband in business and a conspicuously idle yet fabulously coiffured wife signified all was well at work. The sobriety of the businessman, with his neat, rather more understated hair, oozed respectability.

By the mid-nineteenth century a new class of literate, domesticated middle-class women had been created, new technologies reproduced images of a culturally appropriate appearance and the construction of woman as the decorative sex, prey to the whims and vagaries of fashion in a way that men were not, became popular. At the beginning of the century women's hair had been relatively short, drawn back in a bun in a simple Greek style, but as time went on styles became longer and more elaborate. With a husband as

MISS BILLIE BURKE.

**Miss Billie Burke,
c. 1900s**

A remarkable head of hair

provider, women displayed their family's status through opulent personal adornment and leisured lifestyles and hairstyles played a part in the creation of this image. Quantity rather than quality became the most important aspect of a woman's hair and mothers spoke with pride of their daughter's hair being waist length or 'so long they could sit on it'. This cultural stereotyping meant that long hair was worn by almost all women across the classes and was the supreme symbol of femininity — one popular aphorism of the time stated, 'With a veil of long hair covering her shoulders, a plain woman may look a goddess; without hair; she is not even a woman.' Little girls were initiated into this aspect of their appearance through fairy tales, folklore and 'common sense', with some doctors going as far as to state that to cut women's hair would increase headaches and neuralgia and subject them to heavy colds in the head. It would have been difficult to react against such a pervasive stereotype of femininity as Rapunzel, who let down her golden hair to allow her prince to rescue her, or the celebrated beauties of the day like Ellen Terry or Billy Burke, and Victorian girls were taught to care almost to the point of obsession about their locks. Giving one hundred strokes of the brush from the scalp to the ends every night was a prerequisite for a successful head of hair. This practice, which would now be frowned upon as making the hair greasy by overstimulating the sebaceous glands, was believed in the nineteenth century to promote hair growth and more prosaically to get rid of dust. As Erasmus Wilson stated in 1853, 'You cannot brush the head too much', but women were warned not to brush their hair immediately after getting up or after eating as this kind of overexertion could be dangerous for their delicate

17

constitutions. Brushes also had to be thoroughly cleaned with ammonia and water after use.

The maid dressed hair in the privacy of a lady's boudoir. She did not venture out to a salon — they did not exist for women for most of the nineteenth century and anyway, a woman's space was very restricted. The middle-class lady's sense of etiquette meant that she had to be accompanied wherever she went, usually by a male relative or chaperone, for the city street was considered to be very much the preserve of the prostitute. It was to the new department stores that a lady could safely go; a conglomeration of small shops under one roof, including by the early twentieth century a ladies' hairdressing establishment or beauty court. Here things of an intimate nature could be practised away from the prying eyes of the hoi polloi. This included the 'letting down' of hair, which was considered a very private activity, in part due to the traditional associations of cascading hair with sexual temptation. The figure of the femme fatale surrounded by a lure of hair like a baleful Medusa was capitalized upon within the representation of women in Art Nouveau, reinforcing the sexualization of long hair and even inspiring hair-styles. This underlying belief is still symbolized in twentieth-century culture by the traditional practice of Orthodox Jewish women covering their hair after marriage whenever in public by scarves, hats or wigs. As the Victorian woman entered adulthood and thus a more public sexual maturity, her hair was safely upswept to show a distinction between the girl and the woman, and hair played an important symbolic role in this transitional period.

For most of the Victorian era women's styles tended to be variations on the bun or chignon, although by the 1870s these

'Art Nouveau', 1903, by Mons. Dupont (Paris)

Extravagant Victorian hairstyle using pads and false pieces

looks were regarded as desperately outmoded and even ugly, particularly if made up of false hair. One writer went so far as to describe the chignon as a 'tumour-like excrescence [which] disfigures the top of the head with the appearance of a horrid growth of disease which would seem to call for the knife of a surgeon did we not know that it could be placed or displaced

19

at the will of the wearer'.[1]

By the Edwardian era an extravagant femininity was rife amongst upper and middle-class women. It was a time of social upheaval, the last gasp of the British Empire, which would have repercussions throughout the twentieth century. The feminine ideal called for enormous hair-dos, padded out to increase their bulk and requiring the administrations of a maid throughout the day. Lady Violet Hardy wrote of 'Enormous hats often poised on a pyramid of hair, which if not possessed, was supplied, pads under the hair to puff it out were universal and made heads unnaturally big. This entailed innumerable hairpins. My sister and I were amazed to see how much false hair and pads were shed at "brushing time". Mama adopted a mass of curled fringe, which was called a "front", made fashionable by Queen Alexandra. In most cases it was disfiguring and very unhygienic, and as make-up was scarcely ever worn, it created a hardness to the face and a top-heaviness which was most unbecoming.'[2]

Extravagant hair-styles such as these were a mark of conspicuous consumption: they showed through their complexity that much time had been taken up in their construction and time meant money, a signifier of a successful middle-class life. A complex language was attached to the ornamentation of hair: shells were used for dinner or the theatre, ribbons with flowers and laces for balls and parties, and fancy feathers and diamonds for gala and royal festivals. The demand for the services of a hairdresser was so great before some of these important functions that many women had to have their hair dressed from up to two days in advance, so nights had to be spent sitting up in a chair in order not to crush the elaborate coiffure. The building of

[1] Richard Corson, FASHIONS IN HAIR, (London, Peter Owen, 1965), p.488

[2] Lady Violet Hardy, AS IT WAS, (London, Christopher Johnson, 1958), p.79

Elaborate Edwardian hairdressing

such massive hair-styles was very much dependent on the use of *postiche*, the French word for 'added hair', and an important function of the hairdressing salon was the work of the *posticheur*, who added hairpieces or transformations such as wigs, fringes, fronts and switches, hair pads, pompadour rolls and frizettes. Hair-styles using *postiches* needed a lot of time and energy spent on their upkeep, so many hours were devoted to brushing, drying and dressing the hair and then filling the style out with false pieces which had to be pinned, combed and braided. Thus hair was dressed rather than cut, which accounted for the naming of the profession; cutting was to come later.

Dressed hair with transformations, c. 1900s

Edwardian hairstyles c. 1900s

Most hairdressers had a workroom in which
were made for sale and to order, and this is w
prospective hairdresser first learned to handle and
feel of hair before dealing with living customers. On
main tasks of the *posticheur* was to prepare, clean an
up hair combings. These were bits of loose hair remo
the salon by the hairdresser or collected at home by a
who wanted a hairpiece. The accumulated hair resemble
sort of scrubby bits which are left in a hairbrush a
brushing and sometimes took years to accumulate, as a re
being rather matted, tangled and dusty. It seems impossi
now that anything could be made from them, but combin
were regularly transformed into tails and switches. Shake
free of dust in the open air, the combings were teased out by
the fingers of the *posticheur* and then disentangled by
carding using a hackle or wire brush. Indiscriminate carding
could result in torn, bleeding fingers but the main drawback
came from nits, which had to be systematically squashed in a
nitting machine. The pieces of hair were then woven into an
appropriate form.

Women not able to afford the expenses of the salon had
struggle with the construction of their own towering hair-
. Cecil Beaton described the problems encountered by his
ther who with no maid to help her was usually obliged to
ss her own hair. He described it as being worn wide at the
es, stuffed out with pads and garnished with amber,
rtoise-shell, or imitation diamond combs. On black
ondays, after a long solitary session with her arms raised,
utting the waves and curls into place, the effect might still
ot please her. Then she would take out the rats, glancing
vith alarm into the looking glass as the whole business
tarted over again. Her face became flushed, her arms would
be aching, and by the time she had finished she was more
than late for dinner.[1]

[1] Mary Trasko, A HISTORY
OF EXTRAORDINARY HAIR:
DARING DO'S, (Paris,
Flammarion, 1994),
p.105

The hair of working-class women was used to provide the
transformations for the crowning glory of the wealthy
woman's head. Hair was a commodity to be exploited and for
many was better than the alternatives of begging or
prostitution as a way of earning income. A famous source was
the Hair Market at Morlans in the Pyrenees, although similar
hiring fairs were held in Britain where hairdressers went in

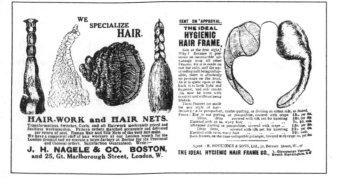

**Advertisements for
hair work and hair nets
1909**

Advertisements for the latest styles in hair frames, 1913

LATEST STYLES IN HAIR FRAMES.

Hair Frames Bound with Silk Galloon, best Spring Wire, Mohair or Crepe Covered.

If you are not at present holding a stock of the above and our various other shapes in bound edged Hair Frames we shall be pleased to send Samples on Application.

OSBORNE, GARRETT & CO., London and Birmingham.

Human hair flowing wig, 1892

HUMAN HAIR FLOWING WIG.

A CHEAP LINE
IN

TAILS

			PER DOZ.
¾-oz., 14-in. Hair	...		**11/6**
1-oz., 16-in. „	...		**19/-**
1¼-oz., 16-in. „	...		**24/-**
1¼-oz., 18-in. „	...		**30/-**
1½-oz., 18-in. „	...		**42/-**

Put up, one dozen in a Parcel, Assorted Colours.

Colours—Golden, Auburn, Red, Assorted, &c., 10/6 each.
LONGER HAIR, 18/- 25/- 30/- each.
MADE IN COLOURS TO ORDER.
OSBORNE. GARRETT, & Co., London.

Patterns not Matched at these Prices.

OSBORNE, GARRETT & CO., LONDON.

Hairstyles with transformations c. 1880s

order to buy the hair of peasant girls or domestic servants literally from their heads. The dealers wandered up and down the narrow high street while the sellers stood in doorways, as 'The hair is let down, the tresses combed out, and the dealer names his price. If a bargain is struck, the dealer lays the money in the open palm of the seller, applies his shears, and in a minute the long tresses fall on the floor. The purchaser rolls up the tresses, places them in paper, and thrusts them into his pocket. It is very rarely that a maiden can contemplate her fallen tresses disappear into the dealer's pocket without a gush of tears; but she consoles herself by exclaiming, "Well, it will grow again," and by looking at the money in her hands.'[1] Most hair, however, was imported via Marseilles from Asia Minor, India, China and Japan and boiled in diluted nitric acid to remove the original colour – a practice which ruined the health of the workers responsible – and then dyed to the most fashionable tint of the day. It was also rid of vermin, a selling point flagged up in the 1880s by Osbourne, Garrett and Co. who advertised a special quantity of hair for sale, 'perfectly clubbed, clean and free from nits'. Attitudes of the time to the buying of 'foreign' hair display the rather rampantly racist attitude to other climes that was inherent in British society. Black hair was regarded as somehow problematical and uncivilized, 'closer to beast than man', and this idea had held sway as far back as 1882, as can be seen in this description in the *Hairdressers' Weekly Journal* of that year: 'The woolly hair of the negro is perhaps to be accounted for by the extreme dryness of the air, which, operating through several thousand years, has in the interior of Africa changed the hair into a kind of coarse wool. There is a story of a man whose beard, while in Europe,

[1] HAIRDRESSERS' WEEKLY JOURNAL, 24 June 1882, p.120

was soft and almost straight, but immediately on his arrival at Alexandria began to curl, to grow crisp and coarse, and before he reached Es-Souan resembled the hair of a rabbit to the touch, and was disposed in ringlets about the chin.'

[1] HAIRDRESSERS' WEEKLY JOURNAL, 8 July 1882, p. 151

Africa was thus mythologized as an exotic, distant, dangerous place, a harbinger of death and disease, where the unwary traveller could be fundamentally changed, and subsequently any product emanating from its shores was to be treated with caution. In 1877 the *Bazar Book of Decorum* warned against hairpieces or transformations which had been imported from the dark continent or 'Caffreland' 'where [the hair] is cut from the heads of the filthiest and most disgusting population in the world. The Hottentot product is shipped to London, near which there is a place where it was purified. This, however, in consequence of the intolerable stench, has been indicted as a nuisance.'

[2] Corson, FASHIONS IN HAIR, (London, Peter Owen, 1965), p.488

The poor white girl's sacrifice of her beautiful long hair had quite different associations and became a subject of debate, prompting fictional accounts such as when Jo sells her tresses in the popular novel *Little Women* and maudlin homilies such as *A Friend in Need*:

'A poor girl with beautiful hair, went to the barber to sell it. He tried to make a close bargain, saying hair was plentiful this year, and declared he could only give her eight florins. The little maiden's eyes filled with tears, and she hesitated a moment, while threading her fingers through her chestnut locks. Finally she said, 'then take it quickly.' The barber was about to cut off the tresses when a gentleman sitting in one of the chairs interrupted him, and he spoke to the girl. 'My child,' said he, 'why do you sell your beautiful hair?' 'My mother has been nearly five months ill. I cannot work hard enough to support us. Everything has been sold or pawned, and there is not a penny in the house.' 'No, no, my child; if that is the case I will buy your hair, and give you one hundred florins for it.' He gave the poor girl the note, the sight of which dried her tears, and he took up the barber's shears. Taking the locks in his hand, he selected the longest hair, cut it off, and put it carefully in his pocket-book, thus paying one hundred florins for a single hair. He took the poor girl's address, in case he should want to buy another at the same rate.'[1]

[1] HAIRDRESSERS' WEEKLY JOURNAL, 20 May 1882, p.40

For men hair was supposed to pose no real problem. It was just something that was there and had to be dealt with as quickly and neatly as possible without too much fuss: this was the orthodoxy of masculine hair-styling. The introduction of hair clippers in 1879 helped develop the vogue for very short cuts — some men had been known to use horse clippers to achieve the desired close-cropped effect — and the Bressant clipper became the model favoured by British barbers. Gradually as the century progressed men's hair became shorter and simpler and looking after one's own hair at home began to become the norm for men, helped by advances in technology such as the mechanization of the comb industry. In 1882 cutting machinery took over from hand production and moulding processes using vulcanite and xylonite made combs less expensive.

In the late nineteenth century a profusion of well-cared-for hair was seen as a woman's prerogative and thus had strong associations with fashionable femininity. Thus for a man to sport a long hair-style was to go against the grain of his sex and the correct length of hair for men became a subject of great contention; for example, long hair was described by the

[1] THE HABITS OF GOOD SOCIETY: A HANDBOOK OF ETIQUETTE FOR LADIES AND GENTLEMEN, (London, J. Hogg and Sons, 1859, Anon)

[2] W. S. Gilbert, 'The Aesthete' in THE BAB BALLADS, (London, Macmillan, 1953), p. 271

author of THE HABITS OF GOOD SOCIETY,[1] a popular book on etiquette, as the preserve of only 'painters and fiddlers', or rather dubious 'artistic' types. The long aesthetic styles of the 1870s and 1880s were ridiculed by the press and public alike and were regarded as the preserve of rather effete men such as Oscar Wilde, who wore long hair and 'walked down Piccadilly with a poppy or a lily in (his) medieval hand.'[2] Consequently young men with these rather avant-garde hair-styles were criticized for putting too much effort into their appearance, intimating a well developed sense of vanity, a trait usually associated with the feminine condition. This was recognized in THE HABITS OF GOOD SOCIETY, which saw long hair on men as 'inconvenient and a temptation to vanity, while its arrangement would demand an amount of time and attention which is unworthy of a man'. Too short a haircut, however, had different associations, those of poverty, prison and the poorhouse, where hair was customarily shaved to get rid of vermin. The hair of fever patients was also cut off to prevent the hair from 'falling' and the roots rubbed with rum and water. Short hair was thus rather unromantic.

The styling of one's hair in too obvious a way for a man was an act causing great debate and, because of the need to tread carefully around these issues, attempts were made to assert masculinity within the confines of the barbershop to deliberately disavow any notions of femininity. Consequently barbershops were, and to some extent still are, deliberately anti-feminine institutions asserting an active male sexuality, the 'something for the weekend' aesthetic. These are masculine arenas of short back and sides haircuts and, before the invention of the Gillette safety razor in 1895 and the self-shaving revolution, the place to find a hot shave. The barber

Oscar Wilde

would soften the client's beard first with a mixture of soap and water, oil, fat or Vaseline using a hog bristle brush and then shave him using a well-stropped cutthroat razor, a serious business with essential rules and regulations laid down to ensure good practice, not least a sharp blade and a steady hand.

Men did wear wigs in the nineteenth century and worried about baldness just as much as their twentieth-century counterparts. Baldness was thought to occur for a variety of reasons: brushing the hair too briskly for too long, an overenthusiatic application of bear's grease which 'rotted the roots' or more flatteringly because the hair had been 'burnt out' through brainpower. 'Grass doesn't grow on a busy street' was a popular rejoinder from a baldie. Mr William Maurer in a lecture on trichology in 1913 even attributed the effects of music to some instances of hair loss and observed that 'pianists, violinists, and players on strings were usually well covered; while players on brass, requiring more energy to operate, were subject to hair loss'. In women 'falling' or thinning hair was believed to be due to the dangerous practice of exposure to evening mists and they were counselled to beware venturing into the garden at night without covering their heads with a pretty scarf. The Edwardian fashion for large hats was also seen as especially injurious. One West End specialist wrote, 'As grass turns yellow under a mushroom, so women's hair will lose its colour and deteriorate under the gigantic hats which are now the mode. There is every possibility of the fair sex going bald unless a revolution in hats is effected. First of all these enormous mountains of millinery shut out the health-giving sun and air. Secondly they present such vast surfaces to the wind that they tug against the detaining hat pins like a kite on a string.'[1] If thinning did occur the best remedy was to rub the roots with salt to puff the hair out, a practice which must have led to many a raw scalp, but more generally the condition was thought to be bad for the health, making those afflicted prey to colds, catarrh and neuralgia. Bald men were also social pariahs, one writer complaining, 'A bald headed man in an audience near a window is a nuisance. When others want the window open to secure ventilation, he, in consideration for his bald pate, wants the window shut. If he puts on his hat, nobody sees that he does it because he is bald, and he is thought unmannerly.'[2]

So did one conceal or reveal the curse of hair loss? The tendency towards disguise through the use of wigs or a skull cap was considered rather old-fashioned by the late nineteenth century. Rudimentary experiments were made in the direction of hair transplants in 1910 by Dr Popovics of Hungary, who sank small hooks of gold wire directly into the skin of the scalp, which had been numbed by novocaine, and then attached single hairs. Up to four hundred hairs could be

[1] HAIRDRESSERS' WEEKLY JOURNAL, 16 July 1910, p. 1118

[2] HAIRDRESSERS' WEEKLY JOURNAL, 10 June 1882, p.87

**Dr Popovics's
instrument for hair
transplanting, 1910**

inplanted in this way in one sitting and Popovics
recommended at least forty attempts for a full head of hair
unless, as he put it, the hairs were long and could be combed
across a bald head. Of course this treatment was spectacularly
unsuccessful and the end result tended to be inflammation of
the scalp and suppuration at the point of contact of the hair
with the skin. It wasn't until Norman Orenteich's
developments in hair-transplant techniques in the 1970s that
the treatment was taken seriously by male consumers.

Hair suffering was not contained just to men. The quality of
the actual mass of hair which made up women's huge, heavy
styles looked and felt ugly. Criticisms began to be levelled at
the malodorous practices which were ruining its appearance
and backcombing or 'frizzing' was seen as one of the main
culprits in the ruination of hair health. Octave Uzanne
complained in 1887 of hair 'uncombed, flutter[ing] in dismay,
mixed with shams of every sort, burnt by acid, roasted by
iron, dried up by ammonia; this dead hair, which fell in curls
or frisettes under the cap, was indeed the most disagreeable
thing'.[1] Hairdressers attempted to educate their customers
but the trade was still in its infancy and not that much was
actually known about general hair care. It was particularly
difficult to clean and dry such huge amounts before the days
of soapless shampoos and electric hair-dryers, so the
practice of dry-shampooing became the norm in the late
nineteenth century: a cleansing agent was massaged into the

[1] Trasko, p.102

hair and the resulting dirt rubbed out with a towel. It's incredible to think of now, but the most common cleansing agent used by hairdressers during this period was petrol. Petroleum hair wash, *Antiseptique Liquide* or, more aptly in view of what happened to some women, *Le Fin de Siècle* was used to clear grease from hair right up to the turn of the century, until several accidents, some fatal, led to hairdressers realizing it was too risky a substance to be used with any success in the salon. As the *Hairdressers' Weekly Journal* warned in 1897, 'This vapour flashes or fires on contact with light, fire or electricity, not only in the immediate vicinity of the liquid but at considerable distances therefrom. Being heavier than atmospheric air, the vapour will, under favourable conditions, travel or flow considerable distances; and it has been known to ignite at over forty feet from the point from which it proceeded.' This flame-throwing effect had led to the demise of several women in London and Paris, including the actress Mademoiselle Pascaline – known on the stage as Irène-Musa – who was burned so badly through an accident whilst she was having her hair dressed that she died from the effects. She was only twenty-eight, having made her stage début when still very young, and had been performing at various Paris theatres. Having consented to appear at a charity performance, she sent for a hairdresser, and whilst he was applying a lotion of petrol some drops fell onto a stove nearby and set fire to her clothes and hair. The report read: 'Unable to put out the flames, which had also caught the hairdresser, Mademoiselle Musa attempted to throw herself out of the window, but her sister and a friend came and caught her by the feet just as she was about to fall from a height of several storeys. The flames

[1] HAIRDRESSERS' WEEKLY JOURNAL, July 31 1897, p. 543

Advertisement for Petroleum Hair wash, 1890

were not put out until her whole body was practically a mass of burns. The hairdresser was also badly burned and both were conveyed to the hospital. Little hope was entertained of saving her and, in fact, after lingering in a terrible agony for about ten hours, the unfortunate actress expired.'[1] A similar case was reported in England with the demise of a Mrs Samuelson at the fashionable hairdressers Monsieur Emile et Cie in London. She had entered the salon to have her hair washed and waved when Mrs Mickelthwaite, another customer standing at the front of the shop, heard an explosive 'boom' and rushed in to find Mrs Samuelson on fire due to a spontaneous combustion of vapour from the wash. The inquest found that the substance was so unstable that it could be ignited merely by the action of rubbing it into the hair and, after the accidental deaths of several more customers, the *Hairdressers' Weekly Journal* took affirmative action, declaring in its pages that 'the application of petroleum spirit to the hair is so exceptionally dangerous that it is hoped perfumers and hairdressers will do their best to discourage the practice'.[2]

Carbon tetrachloride was seen as a suitable replacement for petrol and began to be used extensively in hairdressing salons for dry-shampooing, but unfortunately it also had its drawbacks. The effects of the liquid were very similar to those of chloroform and fatalities occurred, one in the hairdressing department of Harrod's in 1909. The fumes were so deadly that this dry shampoo had to be used in a well-ventilated room with the customer facing an open window. Special basins were invented to catch the dangerous liquid from the back of the head during the procedure and electric fans were used for the double purpose of drying the hair and

[1] HAIRDRESSERS' WEEKLY JOURNAL, 27 February 1909, p.349

Advertisement for Tetra-Chloride of Carbon, 1908

[2] Ibid.

dissipating the fumes. Hairdressers were also advised never to administer carbon tetrachloride to any woman wearing stays and without ascertaining when she had had her last meal. Despite the danger it was still in use at the barbers in the 1930s, presumably because the stronger constitutions of men could withstand its deleterious effects. Foan, a writer of many standard texts for the prospective hairdresser, was still cautious and delivered a warning to the trade in 1931:

Advertisement for Shampoo Basin, c. 1900s

[1] Foan, p.354–5

'In these days of extensive motor transport it is not an uncommon thing for hairdressers to be requested to rid a client's hair and scalp of a thick lubricating oil. The scalps of garage workers and some factory workers become clogged with oil, which, of course, attracts additional dirt, and the hairdresser finds that ordinary shampoo washes fail to cleanse in such cases. He, therefore, turns to carbon tetrachloride, which, of course, proves an excellent cleanser and solvent of grease. Whilst tetrachloride is undoubtedly efficacious as a solvent, it has certain definite drawbacks when used as a shampoo. It gives off an unpleasant odour, which, if inhaled, is dangerous both to the operator and the client. To persons with weak hearts it is most dangerous: in fact, the death of a hairdresser's client has been known to result from its use.'[1]

By this time, however, a more commonsensical attitude had entered into ladies' hairdressing as after the 1914–18 war the vogue for shorter bobbed hair for women commenced. Women were having their hair cut for the first time since the late eighteenth century, when avant-garde women went for the Titus cut, part of the Neoclassical craze which was

35

sweeping Europe. This short, Roman-inspired style was worn with flimsy muslin dresses, dampened so that their folds moulded the body in the mode of the drapery of statues *à l'antique*. There had also been the short-lived fad in the 1880s, for what was called 'close-cutting' which had been debated in the pages of the *Hairdressers' Weekly Journal* whose writer had seen:

'very many girls sacrificing good heads of hair for the sake of a present whim. The London hairdresser leaves a fringe to fall partially over the forehead, but cuts the hair quite close at the back, where it is snipped off as short as a boy's; from the crown to the nape of the neck, nowhere is it more than half-an-inch long. One fashionable hairdresser told me he had shaved off at least a dozen splendid heads of hair within the last fortnight; but I should advise my fair friends to pause before committing women's crowning glory to the barber's basket. Some foolish young friends of mine, who have sacrificed their hair, tell me they have the utmost difficulty in keeping anything on their heads except gear which is adopted by men, such as poke caps and similar coverings. It may be well for those who are contemplating the matter to remember and apply the story of the frogs in the fable, who, before leaping into the well, paused to consider how they should get out of it again.'[1]

[1] THE HAIRDRESSERS' WEEKLY JOURNAL, 28 OCT 1882, p. 410

Warning a young woman who was contemplating 'close-cutting' that she might be able to wear only masculine headgear from then on, was a prophetic intimation of how the bob was to be criticized in the early 1920s, when it was viewed as a look which rather frighteningly blurred the

Close cutting, c.1900

Miss Isobel Elsom

distinctions between male and female. Unlike the bob, however, close-cutting was usually carried out on hair which had become thin as a result of overbinding when tying in *postiches* and too much crimping, curling and dyeing. Up to the 1920s most long hair was never cut, so consequently the bob was rather a challenge to the embryonic trade of the ladies' hairdresser, whose training had been in styling. Women of all classes began having their hair bobbed, not for the price it would bring but for the sake of fashion, and for the first time the quality of hair-dos was determined by cut rather than styling. The enthusiasm for the new style was due to several factors – shorter hair was not only easier to care for but for some it also exemplified everything believed to be modern about the New World Order after the carnage of the First World War. The strictures of the old aristocratic regime were being tossed aside in favour of a modern culture dominated by notions of youth and the hedonism of consumption. The modern woman was busy and didn't have the time to brush and care for her long hair, and new modes of travel such as the car demanded easier-to-care-for styles. Foan astutely recognized this cultural shift, commenting, 'The modern women, with her economic independence, sets out to get her own living, and she does not want to bother attending to long tresses, either night or morning. There is no doubt that our women have never looked so chic, clean and neat, both in head-dress and clothes, than at this period.'[1]

[1] Foan, p.141

The origin of the bob is debatable as it was a originally a non-gendered style for children imported from Vienna to America in the early twentieth century, arriving in Britain around 1910, and was given several names during its evolution, including the American short cut style, Dutch cut

Child's bob, c. 1920s

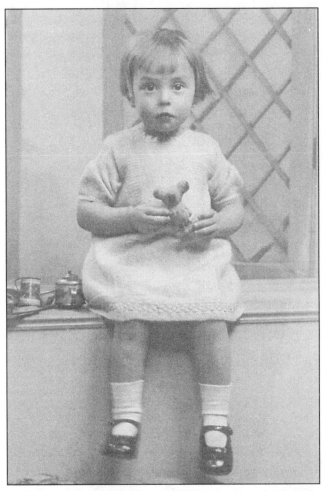

or Buster Brown style. The American version of the look, which was modified by British hairdressers, was popularly worn with an enormous 'Poppa' bow, where the fringe was cut hard across the forehead to the ears, with the ends sheared off as sharply as possible, and the same with the hair

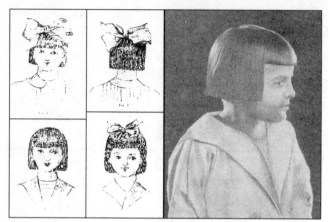

Bobbed hair for children

at the back. The boys' version had to incorporate a much smaller bow, if at all, but the cut was exactly the same. Bobbed hair for children became more and more popular as the century progressed, but a version for women took some time to become generally acceptable. One of the first women to be bobbed was the actress Eve Lavallière, whose hair was cropped for an acting part in 1911 by Antoine, the artist-coiffeur who was based in Paris. Antoine clearly makes reference to the roots of this celebrated haircut when he describes how the new look evolved. At the time the actress was forty-five, about to play the part of an eighteen-year-old and understandably nervous about it. Antoine solved the problem of making her appear younger by using a hair-style which was associated with youth, taking as his inspiration a child whose 'hair was cut short all around her head with bangs that fell nearly into her eyes and a little ribbon on top. As I looked from Lavallière's heavy head of dark hair to the trim, neat, child's silhouette, I had an idea. And I said to her, "A small head looks younger. We've got to make your head

The bob as a universal style symbolizes youth, c. 1920s

[1] Antoine, ANTOINE BY ANTOINE, (London, WH Allen Co. Ltd, 1946), p. 43

smaller. First I'm going to thin out your hair." "Please don't cut it much," she said. "I don't want to look silly." Little by little I snipped off the hair and made bangs across her forehead ... Before the morning was over I had cut her hair into a bob, the first bobbed haircut of this new day, years before any other woman wore a bob.[1] The photograph of Lavallière (overleaf) depicts a hair-style which would not have been recognized as a true bob in the 1920s, being too long and curled at the ends, but in 1911 it caused a sensation. However, the time was still not quite right for the bob to be incorporated into a woman's fashionable look and it wasn't

Eve Lavallière

Hair by Antoine, 1911

until 1912 that Antoine was prepared to cut another. Then,'a bell rang inside my head. The time had come for women to have their hair short. This new automobile in which women sat open to the winds, these new women with careers, this busy life. And these changing clothes, which demanded small, neat heads, not enormous masses of hair.'[1] Hair began to be cut off all around the head, level with the bottom of the ear lobes, a welcome change from all the paraphernalia of pomades and greasy dressings that went with long hair, and the style became very quickly established in the public's

[1] Antoine, p. 45

HAIRDRESSERS' WEEKLY JOURNAL, 1917, 'is ladies hair to be shortened?'

IS LADIES' HAIR TO BE SHORTENED?
TENDENCY IN PARIS TO CUT THE HAIR.   COIFFURES TO SUIT THE
NEW STYLE.

1917 caption in HAIRDRESSERS' WEEKLY JOURNAL 'modern women are not all stupid enough to adopt such a style'

[1] Antoine, p.78

imagination with the new woman or flapper. This was the woman who symbolized the modern era of equality and whose power was beginning to be consolidated through events such as the passing of the *1918 Sex Disqualification Removal Act*, which gave women the right to enter Parliament, and do other public and professional work. The bob was also a response by young women to the democratization of fashion, as it was available for women of all classes to copy relatively cheaply and successfully. It can be seen as one of the first truly widespread hair-dos in Britain, a fact Antoine observed — 'English women took more quickly to the short bob than those of any other nation.'[1] The newness of the new woman was less about her changing role than her changing response to and embracing of fashionable styles which were now increasingly open to her. The *Daily News* in 1921 was one of the first newspapers in London to note the emergence of this new style and included the words of a young woman who was suffering at the hands of some over enthusiastic West End hairdressers, complaining, 'Every time I go to get my hair shampooed, the assistants want to bob my hair.'

At first it was the minority of women who bobbed their hair and long hair continued to be the prevailing fashion, but within a few years the Garçonne or boyish look had taken over. Young women began to flock to the hairdresser's with their mothers in tow. As one observed,' All the young women at the office were having their hair cut short ... my mother and I went to the hairdresser's on Wardour Street, where we sat at the end of a long queue of women who, like us, were patiently waiting to let down their beautiful long hair. An hour later, with hats too large for our diminished heads, feeling very self-conscious, anxious to be home where we could make a minute, pitiless examination of our changed appearance, we emerged as new women.'

[1] Trasko, p.112

A tubular look became the ideal, with short skirts and short hair under a modernistically streamlined cloche hat. Bobs were club-cut to achieve the desired effect, the hair being cut straight along its edges for a blunt look. Styles became increasingly shorter with the shingle, where the back of the head was trimmed closely with the hair falling forward into a bob, then the bingle, a shorter version of the shingle, and then the severe Eton crop, fashionable around 1926, which was cut above the ears and very short at the back. The mingle was another version of the shingle, with curls and waves mingled together in an 'artistic' manner. All these styles were thinned, the hair cut from underneath to give a neat effect: the look to aim for was one of polished sleekness set off with a brilliantined kiss curl. Aldous Huxley described Lucy, a character from his 1923 novel *Point Counterpoint*, as 'blue

'Mingle', 1931

Norma Talmadge with shingle, c. 1920s

Shingle, 1920s

**Josephine Baker
c. 1920s**

round the eyes, a scarlet mouth and the rest dead white against a background of shiny metal-black hair'. The bob for writers like Huxley embodied romantic notions of modernism and Art Deco, the hard-edged design imported from the Bauhaus softened down for public consumption and incorporating the contemporary fad for health, sports and dancing expressed in the fashionable ideal of serpentine slimness. This modernist fashionability is displayed to its greatest effect in Josephine Baker's sleek 'bakerfix' hair-styles of 1920s Paris and her collection of avant-garde wigs designed by the hairdresser Antoine, although it was still the underlying assumption within early black hairdressing in Europe and America that white hair-styles were the norm and black the exotic 'other'. Josephine Baker may have had a hair-style which spoke of contemporary urban life but she was still viewed as a sexualized, primitive 'savage'. Contemporary descriptions of her appearance on stage make much of her animalistic 'blackness', within which her modernist hair-style is almost invisible:

'Her lips were painted black, her skin was the colour of a banana, her short hair was stuck down on to her head and gleamed dully like caviar, her voice was shrill, her body moved in a perpetual trembling and twisting. She grimaced, she tied herself in knots, she limped, she did the splits and finally she left the stage on all fours with her legs stiff and her bottom higher than her head, like a giraffe in old age. Was she horrible, delicious, black, white? She moved so quickly nobody could decide ... Her finale was a barbaric dance ... a triumph of lewdness, a return to prehistoric morality.'

[1] Andrea Stuart, SHOWGIRLS, (London, Jonathan Cape, 1996), p.77

47

By 1926 both hair and skirts had become shorter and the stereotype of the flapper had become part of popular mythology. Cecil Beaton described this new woman in 1928 by simply referring to the new hair-styles of the day and showed

**Rudolph Valentino
with brilliantined hair
c. 1920s**

Androgynous Eton crop, 1920s

Predatory flapper with fringed bob, 1920s

[1] Cecil Beaton, VOGUE, 1928

that men were not exempt from the new looks. 'Our standards are so completely changed from the old that comparison is impossible. We flatten our hair on purpose to make it sleek and silky and to show the shape of our skulls, and it is our supreme object to have a head looking like a wet football on a neck as thin as a governess' hat-pin.'[1] The slick look favoured by men was inspired by Rudolph Valentino in the 1921 film *The Sheik* and sales of brilliantine soared.

But not everyone was as enthusiastic about these changes as the avant-garde Beaton. The associations between long hair and the appropriately feminine look for a woman were so strong, it was understandable that the shearing of it would provoke strong reaction. Short hair on women became synonymous with a different take on the flapper – an assertive unfeminine woman who began to take over from the cute party girl in the public's imagination. This new woman was deemed unnecessary, a superfluous being who embodied male fears about her move away from the traditional roles of mother and homekeeper. The decline in birth rate maintained by the war and the gradual availability of contraception, which began to be used by middle-class married couples, seemed to exemplify this threat. Instead of a patriotic figure who had kept the country going during the war years, the working woman was now seen as a parasite taking jobs at the expense of men and threatening the position of the matron. Beauty books began to exhort the older woman to take note of her perilous position, one stating poignantly, 'No longer is a woman's place only in the home. The war has produced a state where thousands of middle-aged women are at this moment struggling hard in an effort to exist. And that is not all, they have to compete with youthful rivals, which makes the fight more grim.'[1]

The shorn hair of the new woman was seen to be a psychological expression of femininity in crisis. The dearth of men caused by the carnage of the First World War was making it impossible for all women to contemplate marriage, a home, children and a secure future, so in response they

The Eton crop or 'La Garçonne' (top) The Bachelor Girl or Nicole (bottom)

(Left) Eton crop (Right) Curls added to Eton crop for evening wear

[1] A. E. Hanckel, THE BEAUTY CULTURE HANDBOOK, (London, Pitman & Sons, 1935), p. 170

were becoming 'mannish', physically switching gender. Doctors reinforced this belief by warning that the shearing of women's hair could stimulate its growth on other areas of the body, particularly the face, and a picture was painted in the popular press of a truly masculinized woman who had so crossed the gender boundaries that she needed to shave every morning. The Eton crop in particular was seen as a far too exaggerated, masculine-inspired style. Gilbert Foan amongst others believed it to be a fashionable aberration, pointing out, 'The vogue of the Eton crop does not receive the universal approval of womankind. Its votaries are chiefly the fashionable mannequins, their less fashionable, but particularly imitative sisters, and the not too numerous masculine-minded type of woman. Except for occasional lapses, such as the Eton crop, beauty is always sure of a place in the ever-changing hairdressing modes'[1]

[1] Foan , p.162

Foan's description of the masculine-minded woman was a veiled reference to the association in the public's mind with the Eton crop or Garçonne style and the lesbian or 'congenital invert'. This category was created by the sexologist Havelock Ellis and exemplified by figures like Radclyffe Hall, who was described in 1928 as wearing her 'Titian hair in a close Eton crop ... her whole aura is highbrow modernism'.[2] Lesbianism was acceptable to a degree in avant-garde society if the couple aped the heterosexual partnering of man and wife. Thus the butch—femme combination evolved, and the more masculine half of the couple sported the short Eton style in homage to culture's expectations of modern masculinity: a masculine desire was written on the body.

[2] Katrina Rolley, 'Cutting a dash: the dress of Radclyffe Hall and Una Troubridge', in FEMINIST REVIEW, 35, Summer 1990, p. 64

Thus the bob and its associated styles seemed to exemplify all that society feared about the modern woman.

She was becoming educated, entering the workforce in increasing numbers and expressing dissatisfaction with her social position and all this seemed to be reflected in her increasingly 'mannish' appearance. Fears of a similar nature had been expressed in the early 1900s, when the first women to enter the university system were exhorted to beware turning into men, exemplified in particular by the supposed tendency to wear heavy boots. Any shift in the balance of power between the sexes was believed to have the potential to lure women across biological boundaries to blur gender roles and the new haircuts seemed to be yet another manifestation of a sexual response to the shortage of men killed during the Great War. Obviously this populist thinking had its problems, notwithstanding the fact that the bob had been taken up by some fashionable women before the war, particularly those influenced by French couture. Paul Poiret, for example, espoused the look and in 1913 the dancer Irene Castle had introduced a shorter hair-style for women to the American public. Whilst dancing in public shows with her partner, Vernon, the spectators had to duck frequently to escape her flying hair-pins and to prevent this social embarrassment occurring her hair was bobbed to just below her ears, a massive publicity coup at the time but a style not taken up by many women as it was considered rather outré, avant-garde rather than for general consumption.

Flapper hairstyles of the 1920s

By the 1920s, however, this was no mere 'modern hair-style', for according to the right-wing press the haircut was symptomatic of a reverse trend in morality and a decline in society. Bobbed hair was accused of breaking up families, increasing divorce and was barred from the Royal Court by

Dividing long hair for bobbing in Gilbert Foan's THE ART AND CRAFT OF HAIRDRESSING, **(London, New Era, 1931)**

FIG. 138. SHOWING SYSTEM OF DIVIDING LONG HAIR FOR BOBBING

FIG. 140. SHOWING PROGRESS OF BOBBING AFTER SECTION C HAS BEEN CUT, AND SECTION B BROUGHT DOWN READY FOR CUTTING

FIG. 141. SHOWING HAIR BROUGHT DOWN FROM PARTING C, FINAL CUT; ALSO DIRECTIONS OF VARIOUS TYPES OF FRINGES, S R H
Note joint line for length of bob

FIG. 139. LONG HAIR DIVIDED READY FOR SHINGLING

131 METHOD OF TAPERING SUBSECTION OF HAIR FOR SHINGLING

FIG. 132. PROGRESS OF SHINGLE, SHOWING PORTION OF BACK HAIR TAPERED DOWN

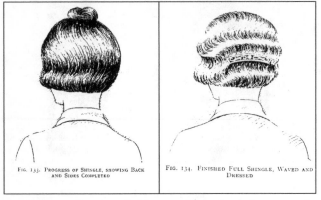

FIG. 133. PROGRESS OF SHINGLE, SHOWING BACK AND SIDES COMPLETED

FIG. 134. FINISHED FULL SHINGLE, WAVED AND DRESSED

How to Shingle in Foan's THE ART AND CRAFT OF HAIRDRESSING, (London, New Era, 1931)

Queen Mary. Despite all this negativity, the bob eventually became so widespread that by the 1930s there were worries that hairdressers would no longer know how to deal with longer hair-styles. Agnes Savill was anxious that ' the modern hairdresser has little opportunity to learn in these days of short or shingled hair'[1] and stressed that correct methods of combing needed to be taught so that tearing out or breaking long hair could be avoided. Hairdressers were also advised to seal off the cut ends of the hair after bobbing with a practice known as singeing. This was supposed to stop the 'juices' of the hair from running out and promote a healthier growth. In THE BEAUTY CULTURE HANDBOOK of 1935, a guide for those wanting to work in a beauty parlour and 'practical help for many ladies anxious to gain a wider knowledge of Beauty Culture', how to singe correctly was painstakingly described:

[1] Agnes Savill, THE HAIR AND SCALP: A CLINICAL STUDY, (London, Edward Arnold & Co., 1935), p. 45

'Twist the tail of hair tightly, hold it in the left hand by the extreme end and, holding a taper near its lighted end in the right hand, commence at the bottom of the strand and run the flame quickly up its entire length, first underneath, and then along the top. As a precaution, place the hair between the second and third fingers of the right hand and slide them along its length in order to extinguish any flame. Proceed all over the head and finish by holding the hair flat and running over the surface with a taper.'[1]

[1] Hanckel, p.20

Shorter hair was not just a fashion for the modern flapper with her redefined role in the inter-war years, it was also conflated with the urban life of the working woman whose attitude towards hair cleansing had begun to change. Up until the 1920s hair had been washed very irregularly due to the scarcity of appropriate cleansing products and hot water. In fact washing the hair and head too often was positively discouraged and it was thought to be harmful to the health to leave the hair wet for too long, so women really only washed their hair when it was about to receive the attentions of the hairdresser. Agnes Savill cited cases in THE HAIR AND SCALP of women 'whose beautiful hair had never been washed since girlhood', not that unusual a proposition for some women, and introduced her doubting readers to a lady 'whose long hair is washed every day; and even after many years it remains in excellent condition',[2] in an attempt to convince them of the benefits of soap shampoos. This notion was slow to catch on, particularly amongst working-class women, who found frequent washing of the hair difficult in communal tubs and whose houses lacked an easy source of hot water. Savill more successfully introduced her readers to the new-fangled idea of washing their hair every month or so, particularly for those living and working in a dirty city atmosphere. This was done using soap and hot water or egg and rainwater and then a rinse of water and lemon juice was applied to cleanse the

[2] Savill, p.52

head of suds and give a shine. A popular product of the time was Hebra's Soap, one part soft soap to two parts alcohol with a touch of spirit and lavender essence, which would seem peculiar to modern tastes because it didn't lather. Hairdressers also used a product entitled Sol Saponis Aethereal, made up of soft soap and ether which had previously been used by surgeons for scrubbing up. Unfortunately the liquid shampoo was inflammable and its use near naked lights could be disastrous. Clients also had to negotiate the widespread problem of ringworm, which was rife amongst the heads of the poor, and were counselled to take their own brushes and combs when they visited the barber or hairdresser because of the risk of infection.

As bobbed hair grew in popularity hairdressers remained aloof, seeing its adoption by young women as a dumbing down of their craft, but gradually the realization dawned that this fashionable shorter style meant that women would be requiring the services of a hairdresser ever more regularly for trimming and thus would end up spending more money. They were absolutely right: the first heroic bob wearers had to brave the barbers for the cut, but eventually the craze for the style led to ladies' hairdressers responding, experiencing a boom and thus a consequent change in status. Women quite simply began to invest more money in their hair. The universality of short hair meant more people had their hair cut in the salon, fewer people wore *postiches*, workrooms became salons and wigs were bought ready made or from specialists. Barbers and hairdressers were forced to improve their methods and modernize. Foan thought the changes had to be for the better:

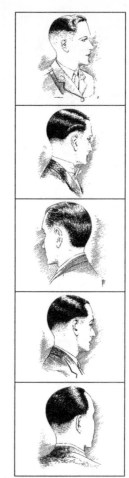

The 'Military', 'Argent', 'Manchester', 'Portland' and 'Arcade' haircuts of the 1930s

Owing primarily to the incidence of the modern short hair fashion for women, the division of the trade into barbers and hairdressers has in practice now ceased to exist. In order to cope with the demand for attention by both sexes, both barbers and hairdressers have engaged more or less in the practice of ladies' hairdressing. The effect of this change has resulted in a levelling up of standards. The barber has of necessity become proficient in ladies' work and the ladies' hairdresser, pure and simple, faced with an encroachment on his domain, has become democratic. The clientele of all hairdressers has become more mixed, as far as social status is concerned. This has been followed by a slight increase in barber's prices and a slight decrease in the prices hitherto charged by the better-class hairdressers. Thus an approximation in social and financial status has been reached, because of the exigencies of hairdressing fashions.[1]

[1] Foan, p.142

It was also in the 1920s that numbers of adverts selling hair creams, after-shave lotions and treatments for balding or greying hair began to be aimed at men. Masculinity was asserted in the names of new gentlemen's hair-styles, such as the Military, Portland and Argent symbolically associating the cut with the upper echelons. The Regent, Professor and Masonic show their allegiances clearly, although most men still opted for an Ordinary — the same cut as last time, just shorter. The cutting of black hair was still regarded as problematical. Gilbert Foan was so concerned that in 1931 he devoted a special section in his handbooks to the appropriate techniques for the budding hairdresser entitled 'Haircutting for Negroes', issuing the following description: 'The majority of negroid types have characteristically close curly hair.

The 'Coif'

The 'Chester'

The 'Regent'

The 'Major' 1930s

Owing to the difficulties usually encountered in cutting the hair of a negro, it is necessary here to offer a few hints to the student. The cutting of a negro's hair should never be attempted dry. The tight curls are almost impossible to comb when in a dry state, and it is quite impossible to use hand clippers in such circumstances.[1] This western view of hair-styling, colonialist in its notions of what constituted the norm, had repercussions on the 'correct' way to style and shape black hair which were to remain the orthodoxy until the late 1960s.

By the 1930s, self-shaving moved by leaps and bounds as a result of the increasing popularity of the Gillette safety razor and general improvements in ordinary razors and strops, although special shaves were still given by hairdressers for important occasions. Fuelled by advertising, the passion was for rush and go, rather than a leisurely time spent at the barber's. A suspicion had also grown up around barber shops that the unfortunate client might find himself the recipient of a 'foul shave', a term used to describe any kind of skin infection which was believed to have its origin from the

[1] Foan, p.96

59

HAIRDRESSERS' WEEKLY
JOURNAL, 27 June 1908

barber's razor and the failure of the barber to adapt to modern conditions of sanitation. Shaving had to be made a more attractive proposition if the barber was to survive; he had to begin to think of himself as a supplier of goods like razors and soap if he was to remain in the marketplace. There was also a general call for the profession to become more progressive to fit in with the national zeitgeist. The way forward was science and by the 1930s its aesthetic had invaded the barbershop with the use of mechanical appliances and treatments such as violet rays, high frequency, sun rays, curative lamps, vibrators and machines for hair cutting, singeing, massage and waving. New

Hairdryer, 1930's

methods of drying the hair other than towelling began to be investigated, including the suction method whereby the air was drawn away from the head, and the more direct blowing action of gas-heated mechanical dryers had found their way into some salons by the mid-1930s, though these were not that highly recommended by those in the know, as the technology was still somewhat primitive. The modern appliances dried the hair too harshly and the fumes which the apparatus gave off were rather perilous to operator and client alike. Those using hair-dryers were warned that during the process they might become fatigued and listless due to the effects of carbon monoxide,

Advertisement for the Blo Electric Hot & Cold Douche Apparatus, 1912

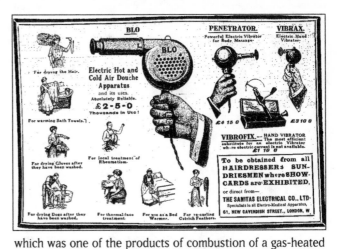

which was one of the products of combustion of a gas-heated dryer. Foan warned that 'after a shampoo, this hot air is blown on the hair and scalp, every breathing pore of the scalp and every live hair is subjected to its harmful effects. The poisonous gas, moreover, is free, and both the operator and the client will suffer as a result of breathing it.'[1] The safer electric hair-dryer had been in existence since the early years of the century but was prohibitively expensive. For instance, one of the first on the market, the Blo Electric Hot and Cold Hair Douche Apparatus of 1912, was two pounds and five shillings and, to persuade the reluctant hairdresser to part with his hard-earned cash, was sold on its myriad uses, recurling ostrich feathers and heating bedclothes being just two of them.

[1] Foan, pp.174–5

As the century progressed procedures grew less perilous in the salon for hairdresser and client alike but another danger lurked, especially for women. This was the spectre of the hairdresser as dictator under whose gimlet eye women withered. Gone was the obsequious servant of the nineteenth century. How had the power relationship changed so dramatically?

(2)

THE
HAIRDRESSER

AS
GU

RU

Before the consolidation of the hairdressing industry, the middle-class man and woman relied on their domestic servants to manage their hair. In fact, Mrs Beeton stated that an essential qualification for a gentleman's valet was to be a good hairdresser; and if a man was not wealthy enough to depend on the attentions of personal servants, the barber carried out the trimming of beards, side-whiskers and moustaches. Barbers had a long lineage and were originally barber-surgeons. Up to the late fourteenth century shaving and surgery were carried out by one and the same person; but gradually the professions began to separate and the barber was only allowed to draw teeth. Surgeons thus regarded anything to do with hair as beneath their station, even though scalp diseases and infestation were common and hair treatments tended to be rather hit and miss, usually acquired from quacks and pedlars. These rudimentary hair preparations and remedies were especially popular if they appeared to originate in France, which was a famed centre for scalp elixirs such as macassar oil, particularly fashionable in the nineteenth century. The greasy mess left from this product led to the use of antimacassars on the backs of chairs for protection throughout the nineteenth century.

In time the position of the surgeon was elevated and the barber began to be seen as a rather lowly figure, the butt of many a music-hall joke. By the late nineteenth century a concerted effort was made by the *Hairdressers' Weekly Journal* to change public attitudes for the better. By then hairdressing was beginning to gain the image of 'artistry' as a result of dressing women's hair as opposed to men's, making the postion of the barber sink lower still. To kick off their campaign the Journal quoted the following 'choice specimen of gross exaggeration and deliberate untruthfulness which has recently made its appearance':

The Average Barber is in a state of perspiration and is greasy; he wears a paper collar; his fingers are pudgy and his nails are in mourning, evidently for some near relation; he snips and snips away, pinching your ears, nipping your eyelashes and your jaw until you think he must have cut off enough hair to fill a mattress. He always says, 'Shampoo, sir?' to which you say, 'No', and he says, 'Eh, sir?' to which you reply, 'No!' two octaves higher. 'Head's very dirty, sah,' to which, if you have experience you respond: 'I always have it so,' and cut off further debate. But he has his revenge. He draws his fingers in a pot of axle grease, scented with musk and age, and before you can define his fearful intent, smears it all over your head, and rubs it in until you look like an animated gunswab. Then he showers weak bay-rum down your back and over your shirt, ingeniously arranges your locks in a way that would make Socrates look like an idiot, and collects his stipend with an air of virtuous condescension.'

[1] HAIRDRESSERS' WEEKLY JOURNAL, 3 June 1882, p.73

The campaign had no immediate effect because the comical figure of the barber as a grisly specimen of lowlife was exacerbated by the belief that hairdressers in general were nothing compared to their French counterparts, and in the nineteenth and early twentieth centuries in particular the main concern for European hairdressers' like *couturiers'* was to overcome the reputation of the skills of the French. The Empress Eugénie made the situation worse by encouraging the hairdressing profession in Paris through her patronage and extravagance and set fashions in hair which were copied by high society across Europe, thus bolstering up the profession. There had also been a band of eminent artist-hairdressers working at the court of Louis XIV in the mid-seventeenth century such as Monsieur Champagne and Léonard, who was renowned for dressing Marie Antoinette's hair, the first hairdresser to use his Christian name, hoping the notion of genius inscribed in the names of Leonardo or Michelangelo would rub off on him. The French were thus regarded as trendsetting coiffeurs as opposed to maids who just dressed hair according to the demands of their mistresses. This sophisticated image of skill and fashionability enraptured women, who were prepared to go to salons with a French air even if it was just down to the name. Even today some older-established salons still survive called René or Paris House.

As the century progressed, calls were made for a more systematic education for hairdressers and the establishment of schools where the subject could be taught. The Hairdresser's Guild was set up in 1882 to 'improve the social position of the trades' through the soliciting of the *Hairdressers' Weekly Journal*, itself conceived in the same year as the mouthpiece of the profession. The first serious investigations into hair health began to be undertaken and with them came the modern understanding of hair and scalp hygiene: the practice of shampooing, for instance, was introduced into Britain by Alfred Tugwell and trichology was established as a new branch of medical science. Science also invaded hair-styling. Joseph Lichtenfeld attempted to popularize 'physiognomical hairdressing', the notion that hair-styles should be fitted to particular face shapes as opposed to being foisted on the hapless client whether it suited them or not. This idea, ignored at the time, was successfully publicized by Antoine in the 1920s and Sassoon in the 1960s. Concerns were also raised for the first time about the employment of children in the trade, a debate which was affecting many workplaces in the nineteenth century as the state took more and more responsibility for its citizens. Examples were given of the capitalization of the young in the barber shop: for example, ten-year-old lather boys who worked a thirty-two-hour week for a few shillings. One case in particular raised public concern, that of a twelve-year-old boy, Harry Hewston, who was charged with attempted suicide.

'The magistrate declared that the boy had broken down under the cruel and wicked hardship of his lot as a lather-boy. On the day which ended so tragically he worked before breakfast, then attended school, returning home in the evening to make ready for his regular employment in a barber's shop. This, it was stated, lasted from six until nine o'clock on four nights a week, and on Saturdays he started at 8.30 a.m and continued until 9 p.m. On April 29th the lad was found hanging in an outhouse, and his life was saved with great difficulty.'[1]

[1] HAIRDRESSERS' WEEKLY JOURNAL, 16 May 1914, p.841

Overwork was believed to be the root of this extreme act. Legislation began to be passed throughout the late nineteenth century and into the twentieth regarding hours, wages and working conditions and this had an effect as the trade began to grow into a big business. The profession of ladies' hairdresser also began to be more solidly established at the end of the nineteenth century and some barbering establishments were far-seeing enough to provide separate salons where women could go and have their hair done

Traditional booth for ladies salon,1924

outside the confines of the Victorian home. One such place was the Don Hairdressing and Toilet Salon in Brighton, which had a ladies' annexe. A special characteristic of this new room was a private arrangement whereby ladies could buy toilet articles 'instead of in a shop where gentlemen might purchase at the same counter, which may not be agreeable or pleasant to the fair sex'[1] and it was pointed out that 'the approach has been most judiciously arranged, inasmuch as the flight of stairs ascending to the salon is reached by a passage leading direct from the street so that ladies will not be subjected to the inconvenience of having to pass through or in fact see the gentlemen's room'.[2] The delicacy attached to gender relations in the salon also applied to the employment of women. Female hairdressers did exist, but had less publicity on the whole. The main drawback was that it wasn't considered the right kind of job for a lady. Madame

[1] HAIRDRESSERS' WEEKLY JOURNAL, 3 June 1882, p.72

[2] Ibid

Martin, one of the first famous female hairdressers, worked at the same time as the artist-coiffeurs in the seventeenth century at the court of Louis XIV, but by the nineteenth century the notion of the angel in the household affected responses to the working woman. The *Hairdressers' Weekly Journal* had a rather schizophrenic attitude to the female barber or hairdresser. In 1886, for instance, it saw hairdressing as the province of women and barbering that of men, asking,'Who keeps up the barber? The adult male population generally. Who is it that stretches out the helping hand to the hairdressers? Women who are too lazy to arrange their own hair, or servant girls who try to imitate their mistresses. O ye hairdressers, leave ladies' work to women, for of a surety it is a woman's job." But by 1890 the magazine was promoting barbering as a profession where women could succeed, lauding the Queen of the Barbers, Mrs Swanson of Thurso, 'who has entered the field almost entirely followed by men and is doing well'. This woman, working in a male-dominated profession, was viewed as a curiosity and her femininity and good character were emphasized above all, as if the appearance of a woman in the salon might besmirch her reputation. Mrs Swanson was thus described as 'a credit to Scottish womanhood, a lady of thirty-two years of age. She is of medium height, not at all thin, has a pair of sparkling black eyes, and wears her dark hair neatly plaited behind. As a rule her dress is a plain navy blue, neatly made, a large white apron, and on her head a dark blue jockey cap. A fur cape is thrown over her shoulders when the weather is cold.' Her delicacy is not in doubt as 'she shaves with a grace quite captivating. No crushing against the bone by blunt razors, no wounding to the effusion of blood. The female barber states

[1] HAIRDRESSERS' WEEKLY JOURNAL, 19 January 1886, p.398

"FON" Electric Hair Dryers
SURPASS ALL OTHERS.

As demonstrated by Mr. Edmund Linenbroker at the Académie Internationale, La Société du Progrès de la Coiffure, the International Hairdressers' Society, and Journeymen's Academy of Hairdressing.

No Gas used. Cost of electric energy is ¼th of a penny for from 5 to 7 minutes' drying of a long and heavy head of hair.

"**Fon**" **Electric Hair Dryers** are designed by a practical ladies' hairdresser, are thoroughly effective, and weigh only about 3 lbs.

They are indispensable to ladies' hairdressers, and on account of their portability and small cost, are **easily retailed**. They give a strong current of air, which may be used cold, or can be heated instantaneously.

In order to quickly introduce this Hair Dryer (which is recognised on the Continent as the best in the market), we have decided to offer the first 500 Dryers at the ridiculously small price of ... ... nett **£3 15s.**

The IMPERIEUX SUPPLY CO., 100, Harrow Road, W.

Advertisement for 'Fon' Electric Hair Dryers, 1909, depicting a woman working in a salon

that since she began to wield the razor she has never given a customer a cut.' Luckily the polarities of gender are not breached by this paragon of virtue for she 'does not allow the cares of her craft to come between her and her families duties. She is a capital housewife.'[1] However, another writer to the journal disagreed about the prowess of the lady barber, stating quite emphatically that it was impossible for a mere woman to give a decent shave. He had visited a lady barber who was 'a very nice young lady indeed but she could not shave. She tried her best; and although the little fingers which seized my nose may have been softer, and have smelled a little sweeter, the fact remains, she could not shave.'[2] Women were too 'little' and thus too delicate to enter such a masculine preserve and men who were prepared to enter toilette salons with female assistants, rumoured to exist in the West End of London, were exhorted to refrain from saying anything about divided skirts as 'Accidents might happen' from sharp razors wielded by 'tall strapping viragoes'[3] — if they *could* shave they must be suffragettes!

[1] HAIRDRESSERS' WEEKLY JOURNAL, 31 May 1890, p.359

[2] HAIRDRESSERS' WEEKLY JOURNAL, 26 April 1890, p. 297

[3] Ibid, p. 297

Mrs Swanson was something of an anomaly at first but with the growth of the ladies' hairdressing trade at the end of the nineteenth century more and more women began to be involved. They tended to have the menial jobs in the salon such as shampooing and drying and a census taken in London at the turn of the century showed that one in ten people in the hairdressing profession were women but as cashiers and assistants rather than stylists.[1] This situation, however, was to change dramatically during the Great War of 1914 to 1918.

[1] Trasko, p.155

As more and more men were called away to army camps for training and eventually to the front lines, fears began to be voiced about how this would affect such a male-dominated industry as hairdressing, by the shortage of both hairdressers and male clients. The situation was exacerbated by the deportation and internment of many foreign hairdressers as aliens and undesirables, a real problem in that the most skilled and successful in the trade were from overseas and had done much to transform the craft into an art. To illustrate how far those from abroad dominated British hairdressing it is necessary only to look at a pre-war survey taken by the City of London Guild of Hairdressers' which identified that of the master hairdressers in London ninety-seven per cent were foreign-born. If all non-British-born hairdressers were to be ejected from the country it would mean closing every salon in every major city. Calls were thus made in trade journals to stop the hounding of foreigners in Britain, but after the sinking of the *Lusitania* in 1915 jingoism reigned and the xenophobia became more and more violent. One of the most virulent campaigners for deportation, the politician Horatio Bottomley, thundered, 'I call for a vendetta, a vendetta against every German in Britain whether naturalized or not ... you cannot naturalize an unnatural beast − a human abortion − a hellish freak. But you can exterminate him',[1] a position applauded in the media. Robert Blatchford wrote in the *Weekly Despatch*, 'To every decent Britain, a German is an unclean dangerous and bloody monster ... It is not only that the Germans are enemies and spies. We loathe them. We feel they pollute the air. We see blood on their hands ... we demand that the wretched creatures be removed. The thought that there are twenty thousand of them walking the streets is enough to make London sick.'[2] Placards appeared in salons staffed by the British with slogans such as 'Is your hairdresser English? If not − why not?' and it was considered deeply unpatriotic to use a French or German hairdresser instead of one home-grown. Rumours abounded of foreign spies posing as barbers who would cut a client's throat at a moment's notice to help the Kaiser win the war. This spectre of the enemy within the salon meant that German hairdressers in particular had to plead their cause in the pages of trade journals. Notices appeared from 'Mr L. Scholz, hairdresser and perfumer, 13 and 14 Pride Hill, Shrewsbury', who stated that 'he ceased to be a German subject nineteen years ago, and became a naturalized British subject in 1895' and the *Hairdressers' Weekly Journal*, a magazine sympathetic to the foreign hairdressers' cause, gave reports of 'five Germans and one Hungarian [who] were recently taken into custody in Eastbourne. One of them (a German), who had resided in the town nearly twenty years, had been employed by a local hairdresser, and had always conducted himself in a highly respectable manner. The provisions of the law, however, had

[1] Marek Kohn, DOPE GIRLS: THE BIRTH OF THE BRITISH DRUG UNDERGROUND, (London, Lawrence and Wishart, 1992), p. 26

[2] Ibid.

[1] HAIRDRESSERS' WEEKLY JOURNAL, 29 August 1915, p.1484

[2] HAIRDRESSERS' WEEKLY JOURNAL, 5 September 1914, p.157

to be carried out to the letter. An armed escort (six men and a sergeant) arrived at Eastbourne, and the prisoners were escorted from the Town Hall to the Railway Station.'[1] One German hairdresser in Edinburgh, Mr Tensfeldt, was rumoured to have been arrested and shot as a spy despite having been naturalized since 1905. To allay his clients' fears he purposely stood at the door of his salon before parading up and down Princes Street and wrote to the trade journals explaining 'I have neither been arrested nor even questioned by any official of any description in the city, and from the first to last these reports are absolutely without a shred of foundation. In fact, I can only account for these rumours by the fact that, in view of the deplorable events that are happening, the nerves of some people in Edinburgh have become jumpy, and they are ready to believe anything.'[2] The populist knee-jerk reaction that left many hairdressers without clients, jobs or prospects as long as the war was to continue left the way open for women to gain a foothold in the salon for the first time. Increasingly they began to shave male clients and cut hair, and an employment bureau for women who sought positions in the trade was set up in Charlotte Street, London. Technical instruction specifically aimed at women was initiated by the London County Council which was to develop into the highly successful Barrett Street Training School, which is still in existence today as part of the London College of Fashion, training hairdressers for the industry. Not all men were happy about this new turn of events, though, one hairdresser writing that women wouldn't take the work seriously enough: 'the institution of these classes might attract a class of girl desirous of becoming proficient in a genteel business, but with no real intention of becoming an employee in the ordinary way — a class of girl hairdresser who, for the sake of mere pin-money, will be willing to give attention at ridiculous rates', adding that 'the economic effect of the competition of women with men in the labour market inevitably tends to cheapen labour and lower wages. There is no satisfactory reason why the London County Council should choose the hairdressing profession in which to dump a supply of labour for which there has been no demand: their action can only result in one thing — a cheapening of the goods.'[1] However, it was soon recognized that the presence of women in the salon could be advantageous and, as the twentieth century progressed, they moved from manicuring, to boardwork, shampooing and drying, until in 1913 'a sympathizer' of the position of women in the hairdressing trade wrote enthusiastically:

[1] HAIRDRESSERS' WEEKLY JOURNAL, 27 February 1915, p. 310

Students being instructed in shampooing 1930s

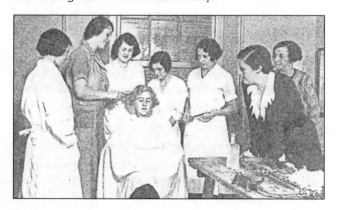

'Much can be learned by merely watching an expert at work' Hairdressing students 1930s

'No hairdresser's establishment today can be carried on efficiently unless there is a female element discernible somewhere. It is not only in the supervision of the cleanliness and comfort of the salons that they make their presence felt, or even in the very necessary laundry and mending departments. A woman can be very useful in many other ways. In the shop many sales would be effected, which otherwise would be lost, if tactfully undertaken by a woman behind the counter. In the salon many a hair order will be taken more easily and readily if handled by a lady assistant. Our customers are ladies, and some of them at least will naturally go out more pleased and satisfied if they are served or attended to by one of their own sex. Living in this progressive age it is absolute folly to think that by attempting to keep ladies out we are really doing ourselves any good. It would be far better to recognize facts as they are, throw all prejudice to the winds, and open wide the doors so that we may reap mutually the full fruit of our labour.'

And women were not just assistants,

'One only needs to take a short train journey to some of our English towns, and in every one there are several establishments where not only are female assistants employed in the ladies' salons, but ladies themselves have actually established and successfully carry on flourishing businesses on their own account.'[1]

As the training of hairdressers in the twentieth century began to be more highly developed and the establishment of a professional industry was consolidated, certain rules began to be laid down regarding personal appearance and behaviour, to differentiate and distance the hairdresser from the barber or 'mere artisan'. Gilbert Foan, in what was to become the standard text for the trainee hairdresser, *The Art and Craft of Hairdressing*, insisted that 'it is essential ... for hairdressing generally, that the student must take special care of his hands and wrists. He must avoid those forms of manual labour, such as engineering, hewing, carpentry etc., which tend to harden the hands, and destroy the suppleness of the wrists. He must value his hands as much as a watchmaker or a pianist does."[1] Care taken in these aspects would hopefully lend an air of refinement to the job and make customers treat members of the profession with a little more respect than they had been hitherto. Scrupulous cleanliness, both of person and of surroundings, was a particular bugbear as many establishments were notoriously filthy hotbeds of disease. West End salons in London were believed to be positively dangerous places to have one's hair washed because of the state of the Victorian drains. Stories abounded of customers who, on being shampooed, were compelled to bend over and bring their faces in close proximity to the hole in the centre of the sink. Any air coming up the pipe formed a large bubble of sewer gas that on bursting led to the hapless customer breathing in its contents. Many salons used fragrances such as rose and jasmine to inspire a sense of security but unfortunately, if the pipes attached to the basins communicated directly with the house drains and thus the sewer, there was danger that the air breathed in by customers could be carrying deadly viruses. To overcome this rather difficult problem the practice came into being in the 1920s of the customer sitting with her back to the sink to have her hair washed.

Even if salons were rather insanitary it was important to give at least a sense of cleanliness. One way to inspire confidence was through dress codes and it was considered important for the gentleman hairdresser to be suitably attired. In the 1930s he was expected to wear a salon coat in white, black or grey with optional coloured facings and always

[1] Foan, p.71

Modern barber's salon, 1907

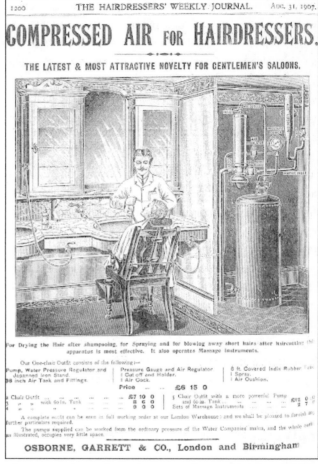

1200 THE HAIRDRESSERS' WEEKLY JOURNAL. Aug. 31, 1907.

COMPRESSED AIR FOR HAIRDRESSERS.

THE LATEST & MOST ATTRACTIVE NOVELTY FOR GENTLEMEN'S SALOONS.

For Drying the Hair after shampooing, for Spraying and for blowing away short hairs after haircutting the apparatus is most effective. It also operates Massage Instruments.

Our One-chair Outfit consists of the following :—

Pump, Water Pressure Regulator and Japanned Iron Stand. 36 inch Air Tank and Fittings.

Pressure Gauge and Air Regulator. 1 Cut off and Holder. 1 Air Cock.

6 ft. Covered India Rubber Tube. 1 Spray. 1 Air Cushion.

Price £6 15 0

2 Chair Outfit	...	...	...	...	...	£7 10 0
3 " with 60 in. Tank	...	...	...	8 6 0
4 " " "	...	...	...	8 0 0

5 Chair Outfit with a more powerful Pump and 60 in. Tank ... £12 0 0 Sets of Massage Instruments ... 2 7 6

A complete outfit can be seen in full working order at our London Warehouse, and we shall be pleased to furnish any further particulars required.

The pumps supplied can be worked from the ordinary pressure of the Water Companies' mains, and the whole outfit, as illustrated, occupies very little space.

OSBORNE, GARRETT & CO., London and Birmingham

observe a sense of correctness in his general appearance. Gilbert Foan advised that the hairdresser's ordinary clothes should 'accord with the general tenor of the profession; that is to say, whilst avoiding the severe, he must dress neatly, always avoiding the flamboyant. A clean collar and neatly arranged necktie are important, clean shoes and tidy, well-attended hair, are important details ... Nothing looks worse than a dirty-looking, frayed-out pair of trousers showing beneath the cleanest salon coat.' The hairdresser had to show he had class and was able to mix with a more upwardly mobile clientele. The impression he hoped to give was that the garrulous barber was becoming extinct and the profession of cutting hair had taken a new turn, so those newly entering the trade were well advised to avoid the temptation to talk too much.

[1] Foan, pp. 71-72

'Undue intimacy or familiarity must be avoided, the student is advised to read good books, to follow intelligently the news in the newspapers, so that he may be able to discuss with his client not only topical questions, but things which are more important and fundamental. The art of good conversation is one to be carefully cultivated. Hairdressers should be able to talk of more than boxing, racing and cup-ties; they should be masters of the arts of conversation and dialectic. Hairdressers have been looked down upon. There must be reasons for this; the hairdresser can eradicate them. The client looks upon haircutting and shaving as a necessary nuisance; let him be shown that it is a pleasurable luxury to which he will look forward ... If hairdressers educate themselves and their clients, there will be a great future for the gentleman's hairdresser. He will be an artist and not looked down upon as 'only a barber'.[2]

[2] Ibid. p.73

By the 1930s the apprenticeship system was one of the standard ways of training a hairdresser. In the first year the apprentice learned what was portentously called the Shampoo Procedure. The 'difficult' tasks started with the correct way of shampooing the hair, how to control the water spray, lathering and finger movement, blotting with the towel

**The art of shampooing,
c. 1900s**

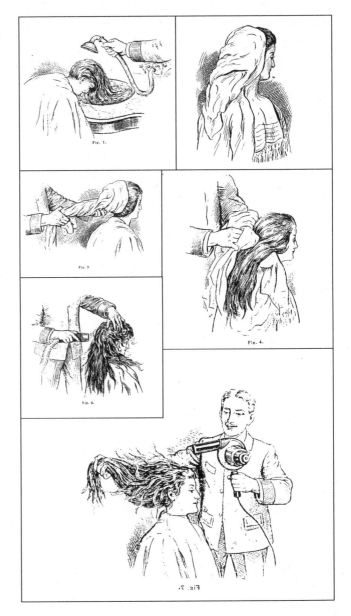

and the combing of the hair from the face. The apprentice also had the responsibility of handing pins, clips and rollers to the operator and putting nets and ear pads in position before the client went under the dryer for a set. In the second year of his indenture the apprentice prepared rinses and bleaches and in the third year began to do a little work on his own. As the decade progressed demands began to be made for a more standardized system of education to substantiate the basic training the apprentice was given in the salon. Technical colleges under the direction of the educational authorities helped reduce the period of apprenticeship and led to a more common standard of training using the City and Guilds system of examination. In London students learned salon work as well as basic accounting, reading and writing and how to speak correctly. Exam papers were divided into ladies' and gentlemen's hairdressing – the ladies' test including Marcel-waving, cutting, singeing and head massage, the men's cutting and shaving. Employers were required to release apprentices for a stated number of hours per week to be given a part-time training which supplemented the education given in the salon. Gilbert Foan enthused over this system in 1931:

'Never before have young entrants into hairdressing had the opportunities and consideration they enjoy today. They owe a big debt to the far-sighted men and women who have fought for so long to establish recognized standards and to help their fellow hairdressers. There may be some who take the short-sighted view that they lose the benefit of the apprentice's services whilst he is at the technical school – forgetting that they gain a more capable, and better-trained, apprentice who will be in a position to start earning money

[1] Ibid. p.7

sooner than by the old method of completely individual training."[1]

In the best known of these, the Barrett Street Training School, pre-vocational training was offered to students over two years, which was considered equal to the three-year apprenticeship in a salon. There were also privately owned schools which had to be recognized by the Hairdressers' Registration Council and further training was available at Academies of Hairdressing, which took up where final apprenticeship exams left off and taught higher skills, a system still in place in businesses such as Vidal Sassoon. This all affected hairdressing as an industry and led to an improvement in the apprenticeship system, which had become notorious as an opportunity for employers to use boys for cheap labour under the guise of a three-year legal indenture. The 1950s brought the two established systems of training together in the day-release scheme.

Salons began to appear, at first in capital cities and bigger towns, then in suburbs and villages, and they often used the name of the top hairdresser of the day, despite having no connections. As hairdressing began to expand so did the democratization of fashionable styles for men and women. More interest began to be taken in the quality of cutting and styling women's hair. There was now more to it than creating the same style for the client day in – day out, that was the province of the barber. The hairdresser could now create new styles and had become an artist; the barbershop was the province of male and thus workmanlike haircutting. The new status of the artist-hairdresser begins to be really asserted in the 1920s with Antoine de Paris, whose self-presentation paved the way for the hairdresser as guru we worship today.

Antoine was a Polish émigré, originally apprenticed to the village *feldscher* or barber-surgeon, and his first duties included the pulling of children's teeth and shaving the heads of the sick. Showing talent for hair design, he was apprenticed to his uncle, Pavel Lewandowski of Lodz, and sent to work dressing hair in the city salon. His first notable coiffure was designed, at the age of seventeen, for the Honourable Stanislawowa Ginsberg of the House of Wielmonza when he was called upon to do her hair because his uncle was too drunk to make the appointment. He proceeded to style it into two long curls or *Schillerlocken* and, as his autobiography tells with rather a lack of self-effacement, she was amazed with the results, exclaiming, 'You are a great artist indeed ... This coiffure is brilliant... I have never looked so well in my life ... This boy is a genius.'[1]

Antoine's stylish self-presentation

[1] Antoine, p.19

Clients began to flock to the salon after such a success, so Antoine decided to move to Paris, which was considered a centre for the hair arts as well as couture. There he worked for Decoux, primarily braiding hairpieces for use with dressed hair-styles, and later at Maître Calloux, where his first innovation was the sculptured curl. Women's hair was dressed very elaborately up to the 1920s and the fundamental problem was that the styles had no real relationship to the head and personality of the wearer. Antoine described the look as like 'an added and unrelated ruching on a dress. Greek psyche knots stuck out grotesquely above or behind gamin faces [and] frizzed bangs hung over strong Roman noses.'[2] Studying the hair on classical sculpture, he was struck by the effects of the neat curls which lay close to the heads

[2] Ibid. p.46

Antoine

**A design by Antoine
in the manner of
Watteau, 1930s**

of the figures and decided to copy the effects in clay to devise
styles which were more moulded and fitted tight to the skull,
incorporating what he described as 'a kind of individualized
wave suited to the form of the face with tips rolled into
curls'.[1] Following Antoine's techniques, the hair was rolled
into flat curls and kept in place with pins, later known as pin

[1] Antoine, p.46

Design of crystal curls with a band of tiny mirrors by Antoine, 1930s

curls, which became part of the daily routine of hair management for women in the 1930s.

When Antoine eventually set up in business on his own in Paris he developed the hairdressing salon into a theatrical experience to which women were prepared to go to be pampered rather than to have the customary job of work

Booths in a typical pre-war salon by Barker Specialities, 1912

done on their hair. This was a revolutionary idea because, before the First World War, beauty salons were dreary places with dark walls, heavy furnishings and little cubbyholes for booths. It was almost as if anything to do with a lady's appearance when performed outside of the home had to be done as discreetly and rapidly as possible. Alternatively the hairdresser would go to the client's house for a private appointment. In his salon at 5 Rue Cambon, Antoine devised something much more appealing for his upper-class and avant-garde clientele. The business had extravagant rooms arranged like private salons in styles such as Empire and Louis XVI. The drama continued with red carpets and peony-red walls lit by Chinese lamps and on the walls were hung the work of modernist painters like Modigliani and the Expressionist Kees Van Dongen. Brilliant red fitted carpets covered the floors – something unknown to modern salons where hair is actually cut off and brushed up throughout the day; in the era of dressed hair, luxuries like these were possible. One of the most imposing rooms had at its centre five washbowls with mirrors arranged in a circle around a fountain of water where customers robed in pale-blue toile peignoirs, rather than the standard drab white or grey sheets that other salons offered, had their shampoo. White lilies and plants in huge pottery bowls were everywhere. In this deliberately artistic atmosphere Antoine, dressed in a white satin frock coat and sporting silver nail varnish, courted notorious women like Sarah Bernhardt and Mata Hari as clients. One of his more outrageous clients was the Marquise de Cassati, who, believing she was the incarnation of a tigress, commanded Antoine to dye her hair in black and tawny streaks to emulate the stripes. He was also the first hairdresser to tint his more elderly female clients' hair pale blue or lilac, carrying out the experiments on his Russian borzoi Dada.

Glass table setting for the Glass House, 1920s

By 1937 the Rue Cambon salon was so successful it had 150 employees, helped by the publicity machine over which Antoine presided, and a branch had been opened in New York at Saks Fifth Avenue. He had by then become a famous figure on the Parisian circuit, an avowed progressive, one of the first hairdressers to use the electric hair-dryer in Europe, and a patron of the luxurious Art Deco style which had swept Paris in the 1920s. The showpiece of his futuristic aesthetic was the Glass House, completed in 1927 on the Rue St Didier. This palace of a rather chi-chi modernism was thought the height of luxury with its glass staircases and walls, and a kitchen that could be cleaned with a garden hose in five minutes. He ate from plates of Bohemian crystal, sat in a glass chair and slept in a glass bed in his living room in the shape of a coffin, which isolated him from the debilitating effects of 'electric rays' in the air. The opening of the Glass House was the occasion of a dazzling party, the invitations engraved on crystal and sent to society figures like Daisy Fellowes, Lady Mendl and Jean Cocteau. The building looked magnificent, decorated with three hundred dozen white lilies especially imported from Holland, and Antoine described 'a dark blue moonlit night when the guests in an unending stream mounted the stairs of glass up to the roof garden where, on long tables, all the fruits of France were laid out ... ten valets in uniform served the champagne. Smiling Antoinettes, all coiffed by myself, offered cigarettes ... the violin mingling with the dark tones of the organ, sent up its sweet melodies ... Through the darkness the fountain, activated by electric light, was shooting flashes of reds and orange, green and violet rays.'[1]

Perhaps Antoine's most famous client was Wallis Simpson, the Duchess of Windsor, whose hair was styled by the master himself on the day of her wedding. Her trademark raven's-wing hair-do, created by one of Antoine's New York assistants, had a flat panel of hair down the centre of the head with a wing-like formation on each side and over each ear and the back simply pinned up. Wallis' beauty needs were rather extravagant even for the 1930s, so much so that one room of her suite at Cannes was converted into a beauty salon where she had her hair dressed three times a day. Antoine was quick to point out that 'this does not mean the ordinary woman's several-times-a-day hair-comb. It means a complete hairdressing by a coiffeur or maid. Each hair-do might require half an hour.'[2] Her daily requests included a simple style to go under a little hat in the morning, a re-styling in the afternoon for a trip to the races, and in the evening a formal upswept style complete with an ornament. Her appearance was dealt with as though it were a military operation, extremely methodical and demanding. For just a

Antoine's glass bed shaped like a coffin, 1920s

[1] Antoine, pp.107–8

Antoine dressed for the white ball

[2] Ibid., p.120

**Madame Butterfly as
Antoine saw her, 1950s**

The hands of Antoine

Inspiration drawn from Nefertiti by Antoine

simple shampoo she had to send out to Antoine's for a specially made concoction of five egg yolks and two jiggers of rum, and on the occasion of her wedding to the Prince of Wales Antoine flew over in his private plane to drop thousands of white lilies from the sky.

Antoine's greatest achievement in hairdressing was the

Antoine in action

abandonment of the nineteenth-century techniques of curling, rolling, twisting and frizzing the client's hair. Instead, he created individual styles suited to the personality of the client. His massive publicity and bohemian lifestyle paved the way for the acceptance of the male hairdresser as more than a mere artisan but someone akin to, if not entirely, an artist.

To this end he was one of the first hairdressers to self-consciously style himself as a genius on a par with the great couturiers of the time such as Coco Chanel and Madeleine Vionnet, seeing hairdressing as an art form like sculpture. Taking great pains in any attendant publicity to show that the roots of his styles were the works of masters of the past, Antoine's autobiography stresses his inspiration from fine art sources in the Louvre. He relates a story of once overhearing his wife, Marie-Berthe, in conversation with an aunt who was confused over the purposes of his visits to the museum: '"Since when," the elderly lady enquired with some malice, "does a hairdresser need the Louvre for curling or arranging women's hair? Look at me, my dear. For twenty years I have been wearing this same hair-do. At least my hairdresser doesn't have to wait for a brainwave before he sets it." "Aunt," Marie-Berthe answered, her voice at high pitch, "Antoine is not just another hairdresser. He is an artist. He gets his inspirations from looking at paintings like those of Velasquez or Botticelli's Venus."' [1]

[1] Antoine, p. 26

By the 1950s France was still considered the epicentre of the hairdressing world, where the incredibly successful company L'Oréal was based. The leading hairdressers of the day lived and worked in Paris, men such as Guillaume, who had been closely associated with the French couture houses Vionnet, Paquin and Mainbocher since the 1930s. He worked with Dior and Balenciaga in the 1950s, creating most famously the styles for the presentation of the New Look or Corolle line designed by Dior in 1947 as a breath of fresh air after the austerity of German occupation, a look seen in Britain as the epitome of Continental glamour after the deprivations of the

Second World War. Alexandre, who trained under Antoine for fifteen years, continued this glamorous trend. However, the era was also marked by the rise of the British hairdressers — Raymond, Freddie French and René — and by the end of the 1950s the domination of men in the hairdressing industry was taken as a matter of course and the standard textbook for the prospective employee, THE CRAFT OF LADIES' HAIRDRESSING, still directed its advice entirely at the young man who wanted to enter the profession. The hairdresser was now a character, an eccentric following the path hewn by Antoine, and hairdressing was regarded entirely as the occupation of extremely effeminate men. It had not always been so. The first male artist-coiffeurs such as Léonard who worked for the French courts in the seventeenth century had been regarded as rogues, Casanova-type figures who leapt on a female client at any opportunity. Contemporary descriptions of Léonard made much of his attitude to female clients, dubbing him 'This scoundrel [who], through his art in hairdressing and in pushing himself forward, was sought after and caressed by all the women. Their weakness for him was such that they put up with a hundred impertinences. Some he left with their hair only half done; to others, he refused after doing only one side of their hair, to finish the job if they did not kiss him.'[1]

[1] Trasko, p.43

The sexual politics of men and women in the workplace had been formerly debated within the context of nineteenth century couture. Charles Fredrick Worth, who was in effect a tradesman, broke down social barriers with his dictatorial attitudes to aristocratic female clients in what was seen by the press and public alike as a highly charged sexual relationship. The public was shocked and titillated by intimate tales of half-dressed women being attended to by a 'bearded' couturier and of a once downtrodden dressmaker dictating the styles women should wear to high society balls instead of being told precisely what to do by his client. This change in hierarchical relationship didn't really enter the hairdressing profession wholesale until the 1920s, with the publicity accorded to figures such as Antoine, and by then the image of the effeminate crimper had been secured which diffused the problems inherent in the intimacy of a man being present when a woman let down her hair and thus, according to sexual traditions, her sexual defences. With an effeminate man attending this highly charged event the relationship between stylist and client was safe, free from sexual misunderstanding, and the presumed ambiguous sexuality of the male hairdresser became a cliché which allowed the intimacy of a man caressing a woman's head and hair in the privacy of the salon. This was only to be overturned much later in the 1960s with figures such as Warren Beatty, the heterosexual sexual predator in the film *Shampoo*. In fact as far back as 1886 aspersions had been cast on the hairdresser's sexuality. As one writer put it, 'Hairdressers, from the effeminate nature of their work in arranging a woman's hair, get into the style of walking, talking and acting like a lady, quite "Jessie", to use a vulgar phrase ... it only requires five hairpins and a petticoat for a hairdresser to be a woman.'[1] Any man wanting to enter the trade was viewed with suspicion by his family but was happily visited by female clients, who had come to expect gay male confidants to cut their hair. Hairdressers developed strategies to cope with these popular notions, realizing that 'the majority of women thought that unless you were both queer and French you could not possibly be a good hairdresser'.[2] Thus Raymond,

[1] HAIRDRESSERS' WEEKLY JOURNAL, 3 July 1886, p. 428

[2] Raymond, THE OUTRAGEOUS AUTOBIOGRAPHY OF TEASIE WEASIE (London, Wyndham Publications Ltd, 1976), p.66

Raymond

the popular British hairdresser permed his hair, wore open sandals displaying painted toenails, varnished his fingernails and adopted an extravagant French accent, even going so far as to have a partnership in a salon in Paris called Desca so that he could bill himself as Raymond of London and Paris. In the salon his assistants answered to French names and were taught to copy his bogus camp persona, even though they were all born and brought up in London. Other hairdressers followed his successful example. Nigel Davies, whilst working at Sassoon's in the 1950s, changed his name to Christian Saint Forget, eventually settling for Justin de Villeneuve in the 1960s and gaining fame as the Svengali-esque manager of Twiggy, the original supermodel. Anne Scott-James parodied the English crimper whose French accent suddenly appeared after a weekend in Le Touquet in her 1953 satire on the world of fashion, IN THE MINK, describing hairdressers who:

'were nearly all megalomaniacs. For some reason best known to themselves they got themselves up as pansies; though they were a home-loving body of men with wives at home and children to boot. They were always exquisitely dressed in nip-waisted suits in subtle shades of green or heather mixture soft tweed, and there was usually a touch of velvet somewhere – a velvet collar, perhaps, or velvet frogging. But if their clothes were cut according to one pattern, the manifestations of their megalomania were varied. One wore a silver-blue wig to cover his egg-bald head. One slept in a suit of armour. One had a blackamoor chauffeur dressed in the eighteenth-century Venetian style. One was ferociously rude. One collected china mice. My favourite hairdresser used to walk around the purlieus of Bond Street with two enormous Dalmatians on a leash which he would caress effusively, calling them 'My pets' or 'My darlings' or 'My loves and doves'.[1]

[1] Ann Scott-James, IN THE MINK, (London, Michael Joseph, 1953), p.80

The flamboyant, wayward genius in the salon, exaggerated in the public's mind by Raymond, was even commented upon in training manuals for the prospective hairdresser: 'Nervous or highly strung persons are a problem. Though one expects temperament to a degree from people with an artistic flair, there must be limits or the whole work of the salon may be upset. These characteristics must therefore be given special consideration.'[2] Raymond was one of the first great eccentrics in the British hairdressing business. Known as Mr Teasie Weasie, his many television appearances made him a household name in the 1950s and 1960s. He cut a dash on the screen with his trademark moustache modelled on the silent-screen actor Adolph Menjou and was ribbed mercilessly by comedians such as Norman Wisdom and Benny Hill. Born Raymond Bessone in 1911 in Soho, London, to an Italian father and a French mother, Raymond learned the barbering trade from his father, who had a small shop with a laboratory in the basement where the family also lived. It was here he invented his own brand of scalp and hair lotions for the barber's shop and no ingredient, however bizarre, was ignored in his quest for new hair treatments. Raymond described summer days when 'he would take us all out to Epping Forest to hunt for ant's nests. He would be armed with a stick and a large Turkish towel. As soon as he found a hill built by the big wood ants he would lay his white towel on the ground and attack the hill with his stick. For some

[2] S.G. Flitman, THE CRAFT OF LADIES' HAIRDRESSING, (London, Odhams, 1959), p.13

extraordinary reason the ants assumed that the towel was the enemy and they would swarm all over it, ejaculating the formic acid from their stings. In no time at all the towel would be wringing wet with the acid, which he would squeeze into bottles. Eventually the liquid would be used to give a sheen to wigs, which in those days were made from the hair sold by poor girls. Usually it was unkempt, greasy and alive with nits. It had to be treated with mercury and washed with his homemade shampoo.'[1]

[1] Raymond, p.16

Raymond went on to study at La Société du Progrès de la Coiffure in Charlotte Street, also colloquially known as the French Academy, which closed in the 1940s. After being sacked by his father for accidentally cutting off a customer's earlobe whilst trimming her hair, he worked in, walked out of or was fired from various salons in London, eventually ending up at Nestlé's. The originators of the permanent wave were based in South Molton Street, where Raymond worked under Vasco, one of the top hairdressers in London in the 1930s, and here he persuaded Vasco to rid the salon of all the traditional, stuffy cubicles to create one of the first open-plan salons in London. His extravagant hair-styling began to be established with the 'plastic look', which had the slogan, 'It goes back into place and is easy to keep', and for the Chelsea Arts Ball he dressed one client's hair to resemble seaweed. His client list included Lady Furness, the Countess Bosdari, who used to model for Hartnell and Molyneux, the Hollywood film stars Paulette Goddard, Fay Wray and Elsa Lanchester, who was blessed with very frizzy hair which regularly needed taming. Despite a loyal following of female clients, Raymond had to find other work to make ends meet and his most bizarre job was as a professional wrestler, dubbed the Masked Stranger, who, sporting a black mask and goatee beard, regularly flattened contestants in the ring. Arguments over his paltry wages forced Raymond to leave for Renato's and together with the Macdonald brothers he put together a crack team of stylists to garner the support he personally needed and publicity for the Macdonalds' new invention of steam permanent-waving. He realized that the way to fame and fortune in the hairdressing world was through the numerous hair competitions which were becoming more and more popular as the industry attempted to style itself as an art. The 1950s was the era of 'artistic' competition hairdressing, a practice which grew out of hair exhibitions given regularly by leading 'hair artists' to show the new season's styles to prospective clients which were created and displayed in a manner akin to the catwalk extravaganzas of haute couture.

Competition hairstyling, prizes for the historical section c. 19th century

Contestants at hairdressing competition, 1903

Hairdressing competition, 1903

One of the first British shows had been held in 1874 at Hulme Town Hall, Manchester 'to show unusual modes of dressing ladies' hair by twelve experts', establishing a tradition which is still followed by stylists today. In the hairdressing competitions many young men and a few women vied for the title of 'Best Apprentice of the Year' and for the qualified hairdresser there were prestigious regional, national and international awards, usually organized by the top operator of the day, Frank Blaschke. By the second year of training the apprentice could enter his or her first junior event, usually sanctioned by the local branches of the General Association of Ladies' Hairdressers and Hairdressing Academies, and academy competitions were held annually for the very best apprentices. The Fellowship of Hair Artists of Great Britain even created a Cadet Force in the 1950s, a unit made up of the more artistically talented young staff, who were trained for international events as well as the national contests, which were held regularly in London, Birmingham and Blackpool, such as the Fellowship of the Hair Artists' Rose Bowl or the Gold Trophy Series. The Gold Cup is still seen as the highest award of the hairdressing trade in Britain and is held every two years by the Incorporated Guild of Hairdressers, Wigmakers and Perfumers. The original competition consisted of a written examination on general trade, technical knowledge and practical work, which included styling with irons, permanent-waving, modern postiche and historical hairdressing. It was obvious that many of the skills required in competitions such as these would never have been used in the everyday business of the salon but were merely attempts to show off the hairdresser's artistic flair. They resulted in peculiar styles and practices being showcased, such as powdered dressings, 'Marcel-waving in the Ancient Greek aureole pattern', and postiche dressing. Exaggerated and glamorized versions of salon styling were created for the evening-wear sections and these amazing fantasy coiffures reached their heights both literally and figuratively in hairdressing competitions in the late 1950s. One example described at an international event was of long hair 'dressed to resemble a highly coloured poke bonnet' and on the same occasion an international competitor placed a small Aeolian harp, made of imitation wood on a light frame, which he had prepared earlier, on top of his model's head. Unfortunately this ingenious piece of whimsy was ignored by the judges whose strict rules would not allow a piece of mere model-making atop a mundane evening style, the accessory had to be incorporated into a more artistic hair-do. Vidal Sassoon, a keen and successful competitor in the 1950s, described the 'competition fever' which used to grip young stylists: 'In those days three or four thousand hairdressers would turn up to watch the competitors at work, despite the fact that the results — particularly the fantasy styling — might never be seen in public. I came third in the Rose Bowl competition, won the Ost Cup for fantasy work and won the Festival of Britain cup at Brighton.'[1]

[1] Sassoon, p.59

1930s competition hairstyle 'The Swan'

**1930s competition
hairstyle with tinsel
and Christmas ball
decoration**

**Competition hairstyle
1930s 'Night: A
Nocturnal Study'**

**Fantasy dressing by
Tom Webb of
Birmingham for
Brussels competition,
1950s**

British fantasy hairdresser Joseph Evangelista c. 1950s

World Championship
Fantasy by Hans
Kammerer, 1958

'Waltz Dream by Herr Bogena of Germany for World Championship in Vienna late 1950s

**Hans Kammerer's
'Die Fledermaus'
fantasy for the Vienna
World cup, 1958**

**World Championship
Fantasy by Fraulein
Rich of Austria, 1958**

**Formalized peacock
hair fantasy by
Fräulein Isborg of
Sweden, 1958**

Raymond's 'Boom' Line of 1960

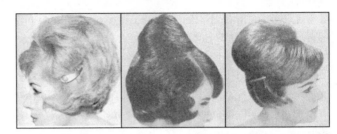

A natural stage performer, using his trademark gold scissors, Raymond won the Grand Prix at the International Competition held at the Palais de Versailles in Paris against one hundred and eighty performers from all over the world. With his winnings he was able to invest in his own business, which opened in 1935 in Grafton Street, Mayfair. Inspired by Antoine's sumptuous French salons where women could enter with the knowledge that they would be pampered and beautified, Raymond created a plush, carpeted retreat with crystal chandeliers, French Empire chairs and a champagne fountain which was used for rinsing hair. Raymond was a master of publicity and, as the decade progressed, the Liberace of hairdressing went from strength to strength, using stunts like dyeing Billy Smart's circus horses rainbow colours. His annual shows, held at the Café de Paris or the Dorchester, became institutions where, flamboyantly dressed in costumes of his own design, he introduced new styles such as the Champagne Bubble Cut of 1956, the Viking Line of 1959 and the Boom Line in 1960. The press and public delighted in displays using floats drawn by Nubian slaves or Christmas trees with girls' heads as the baubles showcasing hair-dos like the Poodle Cut, a look which became one of the most popular of the 1950s where the model's hair was cut very short and then waved and curled. Raymond was also responsible for the reinvention of one of hairdressing's most enduring cuts, the pageboy, styled for the actress Miriam Hopkins. Her blonde hair was extremely fine and was subsequently difficult to handle. Raymond contrived to drape-cut her hair into the style, which was cut into the neck, with the ends in front turned under to form a fringe in the manner of portraits of Renaissance boys. The style was further popularized by Constance Cummings in the film *Three Smart Girls*.

By the mid-1950s the male hairdresser was in full control of even the most recalcitrant client. If one of Raymond's seemed even the least bit wary of what he was proposing he offered what he called a 'temporary wave', which was shorthand for 'Goodbye, there's the door!' Like Antoine before him, he felt women didn't really have a clue about what suited and was best for them — not really that different from how most men viewed women in the 1950s — and it was felt to be to a woman's cost if she ignored the solemn words of her hairdresser. Consequently, Raymond had strong opinions on the subject of who knew best, stating quite categorically, 'The problem with most women is that they cannot visualize a hair-style, so the only answer is to be firm. Tell them they must either agree with what you decide or you will not do their hair. If a woman chatters endlessly I shut her up with a single comment: "Talk is cheap, madam," I say, "but money buys houses, so let's get on with it ... I finish off the job that God left unfinished." [1]

Raymond's essentially camp showmanship, teasie-weasieing his model's hair to the strains of his signature tune, 'Jeannie with the Light Brown Hair', was a parody of self-presentation which was overturned by the march of the new, young designers in the early 1960s, who were influenced by far more serious-minded hairdressers like Freddie French.

[1] Raymond, p.130

A Freddie French style, 1960

Not all members of the profession wanted to be seen in the same way as Raymond and by 1963 letters began to be published in trade magazines such as *Hair and Beauty* criticizing his image and suggesting he was holding hairdressing up to public ridicule. One such missive described Raymond appearing 'on a lively tea-time Midlands programme with a parade of beach-dressed lady models with "op art" sunglasses which got more attention than the geometric door-step haircuts. I can see him now sitting up in the small hours sticking plastic dahlia petals to the protruding sunglasses because its "the thing." But dammit, for his finale he brought on a male model who sported a perm. The guy was coiffed to the eyeballs. But that wasn't all, no sir, he wore op art sunglasses, a collar and tie,

Fantasy by French, 1960

Fantasy by French, 1960

[1] Jimmy O'Neill, 'O'Neill attacks chi-chi', HAIR AND BEAUTY, 1963, p.42

epaulettes and beach shorts with a shirt. Once again Raymond embarrassed me.'[1]

Freddie French was a different breed, an innovator rather than a showman, and was responsible for initiating a new, softer look for women instead of the rigid set hair-styles which had held sway in the 1950s. When he opened his first salon in the 1930s he deliberately refused to install any Marcel or tong-waving points but preferred to set hair-styles by hand to give a softer, more casual look. During the war, when he was in the Royal Air Force, the business had to close but he reopened in Cork Street, London. Vidal Sassoon recalls being in an audience watching French's techniques around this time and hearing people laugh out loud because they thought his new styles and techniques were ridiculous: 'I used to watch Freddie at the Academy. I would stand there enthralled, but, I am sorry to say, I was one of the very few who understood what he was doing. He was so way out, so new, so utterly different ... the audience did not realize that here was a man who was going to change hairdressing, sweep away the set

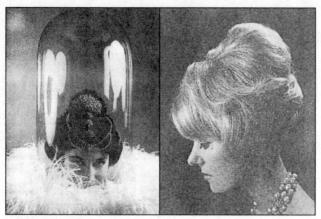

'Showgirl in showcase' by French, 1960

Freddie French, 1960

look and replace it with something soft and simple, fresh, natural and swinging in every sense of the word. At that time clothes were following the movement of the body. Freddie, by brushing hair out, made it flow with the clothes, complementing the mood instead of detracting from it.'[1]

[1] Sassoon, p.69

It was also in the 1950s that women began to move more and more to the fore in the increasingly glamorous hairdressing profession. Famous women stylists and cutters included Maria and Rosy Carita, who were renowned for constructing extravagant fashion wigs and hairpieces and were responsible for Jean Seberg's infamous Left Bank crop in *A Bout de Souffle*. They were very aware of their unusual position. 'We opened the profession to women. Before us, women didn't have the right to be considered grand coiffeurs.'[2] By the early 1960s attitudes to women in the trade and their role in general began to be reflected in comments in contemporary beauty books. Sylvia Duncan, on describing the top hairdressers in London, posed a pointed question: 'A woman's crowning glory is her hair, so why, therefore, should it be mostly men who lead in the field of women's

[2] Ibid., p.122

Styled by Evansky, 1960

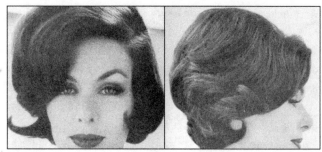

hairdressing — men who excel at gilding the lily? Certainly there are many successful women hairdressers, notably Rose Evansky, but the top list brackets together the names of men, René, Alan Spiers, Raymond, Steiner, Martin Douglas — which is a composite of the names of two brothers, Martin and Douglas. Most of them are middle-aged or older. They came into hairdressing when it hadn't been thought of as a suitable occupation for nice young ladies.'[1]

[1] Eileen Allen, ed, THE BOOK OF BEAUTY, (London, George Newnes Ltd, 1961) p.322

Some inroads were being made by women such as Evansky, who had a successful salon in North Audley Street, London, but it took a man to break the mould — Vidal Sassoon, who was a member of the revolutionary set reacting against establishment values in the 1950s and 1960s. Hair was part and parcel of this change in attitude, from the greasy quiffs of the rebellious teddy boys to the pony tails of girls jiving to the beat of the jukebox. For the first time since the nineteenth century young men in Britain were growing their hair long in response to the short back and sides which had dominated wartime Britain, and as a final act of rebellion before their two years of enforced national service young men grew long extravagant hair-styles based on Hollywood movie stars like Tony Curtis. The introduction of grease had made the quiff a possibility and these extravagant sculptures

Rose Evansky with husband, 1960

were held in place by constant combing and lashings of Nu Nile, Brylcreem or Black and White. Just as David Bailey, a docker's son, was making it in the formerly privileged world of high fashion photography, and Tom Courtney and Alan Bates were breaking the stranglehold of the upper-class vowels of RADA-trained actors, so young hairdressers began to pave the way for a new generation.

Vidal Sassoon was born in 1928 in Shepherd's Bush, London, to a Spanish dancer and a carpet salesman. After his

Tony Curtis, 1950s

parents' separation at the age of four, his mother brought up the family on her own until Sassoon was coerced into the trade of hairdresser, studying under 'Professor' Cohen in the Whitechapel Road, who also trained the hairdressers Rose Evansky and Robert Zackham, owner of a string of successful salons in the 1950s. Sassoon also supplemented his education with evening classes at Regent Street Polytechnic and at the Hairdressing Academy in Charlotte Street. He related his first encounter with Cohen's salon, when on entering the door 'a strange smell swamped my nostrils, a mixture of scent and ammonia. All around me were women, trussed up to the neck in gowns, strange apparatus on their heads, making them look like creatures from outer space.'[1] This was an atmosphere against which he was going to rebel. After learning the trade at a number of salons, including Raymond's, Sassoon opened his first salon at 108 Bond Street in 1954. He was beginning to have very definite ideas about styling hair which were to be revolutionary, interpreting the signs of the times: 'Around me I could see clothes that had a wonderful shape to them and all because of the cutting. I wanted to see hair keeping up with fashion, maybe jumping ahead of it, leading it along a certain line, instead of lagging behind it. I wanted to shape heads, as the new, young fashion designers were shaping bodies. I wanted to cut hair as they cut cloth. I wanted to be in on the revolution that was simmering.'[2] Sassoon rejected the heavily styled and set hair which had dominated fashion in the 1950s and clients asking for Ann Sheridan fringes with duck's tails at the back were turned away from his salon. Using cutting methods learned from Raymond and brushing from Freddie French, he invented entirely new techniques trying to match the new, young styles invented by fashion designers such as

Mary Quant. Fashion shows in the late 1950s presented models very traditionally on the catwalk and hair-styles in particular were very orthodox. Neat chignons, described by Quant as climbing up the back of the head like ivy, were the order of the day, following the rules laid down by couturiers such as Dior for the presentation of the New Look mode of 1947. This simple elegant style had survived for over a decade because it complemented the garments and didn't detract from the purpose of the show, which was to sell clothes; and there was also the old question of cleanliness, as long, loose hair might mark the fabrics. Sassoon decided to break the mould and as Quant sat in the salon he put forward his new idea: 'I'm going to cut the hair like you cut material. No fuss. No ornamentation. Just a neat, clean, swinging line. All I had to do was cut the back short and leave the sides long. I took out a pair of five-inch scissors, which were shorter than many hairdressers use, but I like them. They take me closer to the hair, make me feel as if they are extensions to my fingers. Then I began to cut. Mary said nothing as chunks fell away from her head. Her face in the mirror remained completely expressionless. At last I was finished and stood back. Mary shook her head and her hair danced, clean, neat, alive.'[1]   [1] Sassoon, p.121

The thick, club-cut style of 1963 was the start of many geometric cuts Sassoon was to introduce to the British public and drew massive publicity when it was performed on the actress Nancy Kwan for the film *The Wild Affair* and photographed by Terence Donovan for British and American *Vogue*. The editor, Ailsa Garland, enthused, 'At last hair is going to look like hair again' and devoted a whole page of *Vogue* to the model Grace Coddington sporting a Sassoon cut. Sassoon followed the Quant cut with the V-shaped cut, the asymmetric

'Five-Point' cut by Vidal Sassoon

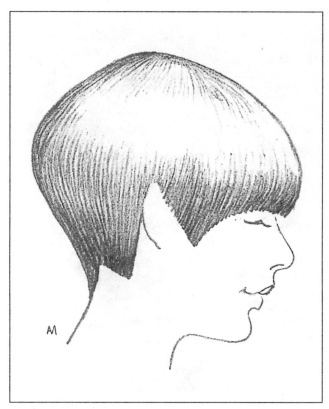

cut (basically the Quant cut with one side shorter than the other), and the five-point cut, perhaps the one which generated the most publicity. This famed style, cut in the salon for Claire Rendlesham, the fashion editor of *Queen* magazine, was created by Sassoon to be the purest, most modernist style he could envisage with Bauhaus principles at its core. Although simple to look at, the cut was a mastery of perfection and intricacy, the five points referring to the two points which framed either side of the face and the other three at the back,

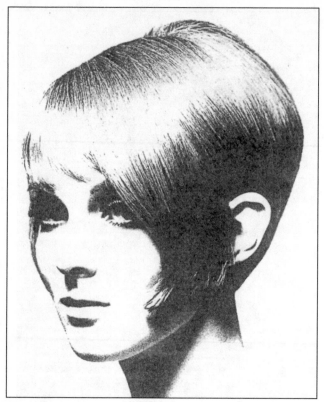

Grace Coddington with hair by Vidal Sassoon. Photographed by Vic Singh for Vogue, 1963

one each side and one at the nape of the neck. However, Claire Rendlesham wasn't entirely convinced at first:

'I'm going to the *Sunday Times* awards tonight,' she said. 'See if you can do something different with me.'

'As a matter of fact I have a new idea,' I said. 'You might as well be the first to sample it.' I don't think she was really listening, but she caught on fast as soon as I got to work with my five-inch scissors.

'Butcher!' she yelled. 'Stop! You're crucifying me! Get

away, you barbarian!' And so on. Even for a journalist, Claire had quite a vocabulary and she pulled all the stops out that day. But, if she had hit me with a bicycle chain I would not have stopped, for suddenly I knew without any doubt that I was on to a winner. So did everybody else in the salon. The stylists stopped work and watched. The customers crowded round in their gowns, catching my excitement. And I kept on cutting, cutting, cutting, while Claire kept on yelling, yelling, yelling.[1]

[1] Sassoon, p.144

Modernist principles were entering hair design once more, thirty years on from the original functional haircut, the bob. Captivated by the work of Bauhaus architects who had settled in America after Hitler's purges, Sassoon applied their philosophies of functionalism and truth to materials to develop a pared-down look for hair, redefining the 1920s bob for a 1960s audience. Sassoon had met Mies van der Rohe in New York in the early 1960s and by following his architectural aesthetic became one of the forerunners of the new wave that was beginning to sweep design, declaring his goal to be the ridding of the superfluous in hair design by paring it right back to the basics. He began to work with the innate properties of hair, unlike other more traditional hairdressers of the late 1950s, who used techniques to change the look and feel of hair. Creating movement was crucial, rather than the normal hair-sprayed severity, an idea underpinned by an obsession with the organic quality of hair itself. Combining this modernist sensibility with a strong notion of what was most suited and flattering to each client's bone structure linked him with the overturning and reworking of established ideas which were revolutionizing all aspects of British design.

The idea that hair-styles should be less independent entities perching atop the head like some bizarre hat and more suited to the personality and face of the wearer, what we take today as an established fact, was seen in the 1960s as a groundbreaking idea. The hairdresser was now a sculptor and the cut was paramount, no longer the foundation of the hair-style but the focus. One of the clichés of hairdressing was invented from this moment on when at the end of a cut Sassoon would ask his client to stand up and shake her hair to see if the style fell into place — anathema to the merchants who peddled the shampoo and set, for whom it was better if the client didn't move her head at all for fear of disturbing the hair-sprayed mass. Not all women jumped on the geometric bandwagon, though, and one of the main criticisms of Sassoon's new styles was the time and cost needed for their upkeep, as the sharp cuts needed a visit to the hairdresser at least once a month to keep looking fabulous. Sassoon countered by explaining that these cuts needed no setting, something for which women had to go to the salon up to three times per week. As he recalled:

'Some women shied away from my short hair-style for quite a while. "It wouldn't end with the cut," they said. "After that I'd have to be in and out of his salon every week, having him fix it for me. Think of the time I'd waste. Think of the money I'd spend ..." In fact the style is so simple that it needs no running repairs that a woman cannot handle herself with a comb. In that way it is more economical than any other cut. It is true that it should be cut regularly, perhaps once a month, for hair that grows quickly. But after that it should fall easily into position and need no setting. That is because the

**Greek goddess-look,
Sassoon, 1967.
Photographed by
Stephen Bobroff**

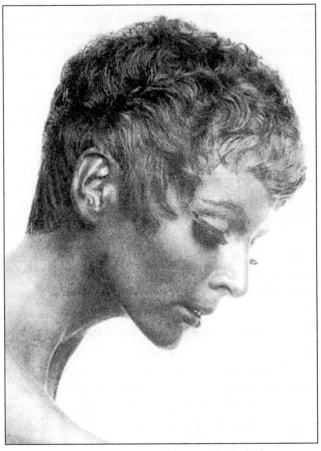

cut follows not only the natural line in which the hair grows,
but the basic structure of the skull.'[1]

[1] Sassoon, p.137

Women had to deal with hair that quite literally felt
different. The idea of neatness, which had been the main goal
of hair-styles since the 1930s, with every stray hair almost
glued in place, was overturned first by Freddie French, then

125

by Sassoon, and a certain casualness began to be the main feel hairdressers and clients aimed for. Women were startled to be told to return to Sassoon's in a month to six weeks, rather than in a few days to have their heavily set hair combed out and restyled, which was the normal routine. In a turnaround from the tradition of mothers introducing daughters to their hairdresser, daughters now brought their mothers in for the latest Sassoon geometric cut, a massive change from the 1940s, when the goal for a young woman was to be an adult 'thirty-five, dressed in black silk and pearls', according to the heroine of Daphne du Maurier's *Rebecca*. The times had changed; post-nineteen a girl was over the hill.

The seeming simplicity of Sassoon's cuts belied great technical skill and hours and hours of experimentation until the style was absoloutely right, following his slogan 'If you don't look good, we don't look good.' There was a sense of play in the constantly evolving forms of his particular brand of modernism, displayed in the asymmetrical cuts which fitted perfectly with the radical designers in Paris such as Pierre Cardin, André Courrèges and Paco Rabanne.The future was now a vision of Utopia expressed in the excitement generated by the space race and new technologies and materials. Thus Sassoon's haircuts were used in the space age collections of Ungaro and he worked closely with the American designer Rudi Gernreich and his muse Peggy Moffitt, who still sports a Sassoon geometric haircut to this day. Every new look created by Sassoon was slavishly followed by the press, who relished developments like the Greek goddess look of 1967, essentially the geometric cut, softened with a perm to give it a less severe, more sculptured look. With traditional perms the ends of the hair were tapered to take up the curl more successfully; Sassoon kept

**Vidal Sassoon with
Mia Farrow, 1967**

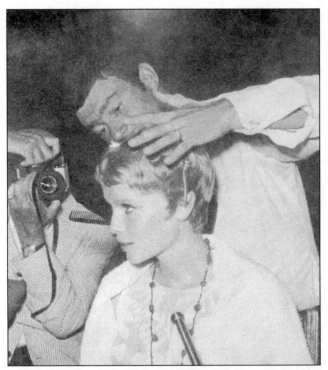

Peggy Moffitt in
Gernreich, hair by
Vidal Sassoon.
Photographed by
William Claxton for
'Queen', 1966

Peggy Moffitt in Sassoon Triangle Point wig, 1966. Photograph by William Claxton

the hair the same thickness from the roots to the shaft and the ends were cut off chunkily, creating a wave that needed no setting. The haircut he gave Mia Farrow for the film *Rosemary's Baby* also caused a furore, this time in America. Despite the publicity, Sassoon admitted he was never responsible for the actual dramatic change of Farrow's hair; she had cut it herself at home and Sassoon was merely there to give her a very expensive trim. At a cost of $5,000 he cropped Farrow's hair; live on a sound stage at Paramount Studios in front of a hundred journalists — the hairdresser as performance artist. He described the occasion:

Somewhere, it sounded as if it was half-way between Stage Thirteen and Heaven — a jazz quartet was playing cool, cool music. Somewhere much nearer the ground a movie camera began to whirl. I put a gown around Mia. I picked up my scissors. I made the first cut, feeling now like a high priest at a royal sacrifice. I don't know what the Paramount boys were expecting when they had erected their little rope barrier. But for once they had not thought big enough. If they had known what was going to happen, they would have laid mines and anti-tank traps. The first lock of Farrow hair had scarcely hit the apron when the Press were down from their seats, across the twenty yards to the ropes, over them and on top of us. They weren't just breathing down my neck. They were damn near breaking it. They crowded and pushed, hung out of the rafters and lay on the floor. And all the time I was dancing round that small, blonde head, snipping here, flicking a comb there, using the ring, jostling and being jostled, while the flash bulbs popped and the jazz band played, unheard now and forgotten. It was a psychedelic scene.[1]

[1] Sassoon, p.9

By the time Vidal Sassoon opened an American salon with Charles of the Ritz in New York in 1965, hairdressers were no longer men who cowed under the demands of their female clients. They were now in control and knew which styles suited them best. The hairdresser was a swinger, one of the most fashionable figures of the London set, soon to be portrayed as a heterosexual sex god by Warren Beatty. Everybody was trying to get in on the act. Just looking at two modes of address from hairdressers to women indicated the change in attitude that had occurred in less than a century. In 1884 this was advice given for the correct way to deal with a difficult female client: 'The customer will frequently require a style of coiffure entirely unsuited to her age and general appearance, and it becomes a most difficult and delicate task to reason her out of this without giving serious offence. But you must do it and do it politely.'[1] By the 1960s this was the mode of address favoured by Twiggy's manager and a former hairdresser, Justin de Villeneuve: 'When a client asked me for a certain hair-style I would ripost, "Sorry, I'm not a faith healer." One client showed me a picture of Brigitte Bardot and asked could I help her? She looked like a buffalo on heat. I gave her the opinion that she needed Billy Graham more than me. Another asked could she wear a fringe? "Yes," said I, "why not down to your chin?"'[2]

By the 1960s a woman was only as chic as her coiffure. Women now feared their hairdressers; they could live or die as fashionable figures under the flashing of their golden shears. The plaintive cry began to be heard echoing across the high street: 'it's nice but it's not really what I had in mind.'

[1] HAIRDRESSERS' WEEKLY JOURNAL, 19 January 1884, p.39

[2] Justin de Villeneuve, AN AFFECTIONATE PUNCH, (London, Sidgwick and Jackson, 1986), p.21

(3)

FROM **TECHNOLOGICAL UTOPIA**

TO **COUNTERCULTURAL ATTACK**

The invention of the permanent wave revolutionized the whole business of hairdressing, although the concept of curling straight hair was not new. Early forms of curling included winding damp strands of hair around metal pins, strips of leather, lead or the traditional curling papers, and pin-curling was a technique used by many women from the 1930s until the late 1950s. In this cheap, relatively easy method hair was wound round the finger and pinned close to

Pincurls, 1920s

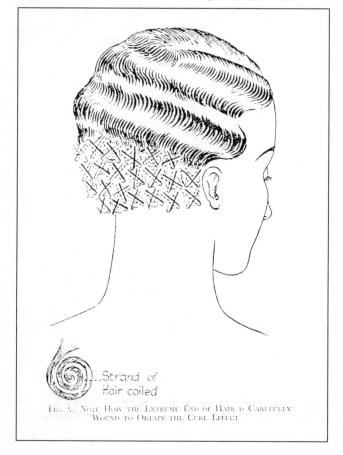

..Strand of
Hair coiled

FIG. 5. NOTE HOW THE EXTREME END OF HAIR IS CAREFULLY
WOUND TO OBTAIN THE CURL EFFECT

the scalp and when the curls were completely dry, the pins were removed and the curl carefully combed out. However, these were all processes that had to be repeated laboriously, usually every night or at least every shampoo, and were considered hopelessly old-fashioned by the 1960s. In the past hairdressers had attempted to give a degree of permanency to curls with the water wave technique where the hair was made completely wet either with water or setting lotion. Waves were set into the hair with the hairdresser's fingers and held in place with a comb, then whilst standing behind the client, the hairdresser laboriously pressed in the set with one hand while the other held the hair-dryer. It could take up to an hour to dry a water wave thoroughly, a process which became less taxing on the hands in the 1930s with the introduction of hooded hair-dryers.

The technique which had the most success, really putting the hairdresser on the map at the turn of the century, was the Marcel wave. The wave imparted by this process was much more successful as its effects could last up to two months or until the client washed her hair. Invented in *fin de siècle* Paris by Marcel Grateau, it became one of the most popular services of the hairdresser and replaced curls and ringlets in women's hair-styles. It consisted of a temporary wave or '*ondulation*' put into the hair by means of heated tongs, a quick, cheap process taking from ten to twenty minutes. In 1872 Grateau, formerly a horse currier, had begun to experiment with curling irons in an attempt to emulate the naturally symmetrical wave of his mother's hair. His indentation or wave was formed by the co-ordination of heated irons and a comb kept parallel with one another, the comb forming the waves and the iron setting them in semi-

Marcel-waving

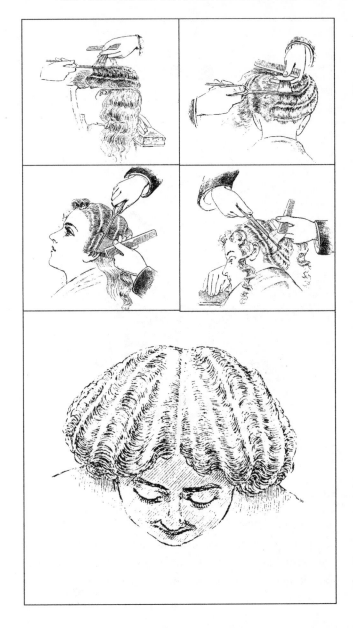

MARCEL

Marcel Grateau, inventor of the Marcel wave

permanent S shapes. The first Marcel waves were given to enthusiastic customers in Grateau's little salon at 87 Rue de Dunkerque in Montmartre, and by 1884 the style had been popularized to such an extent by actresses such as Jane

Hading that Grateau had become a celebrity hair-stylist, fashioning the heads of, amongst others, the actresses Diane de Pougy, Melba and La Belle Otero. As his fame spread his fee increased accordingly, from two francs to five hundred, culminating in Lady Lennox summoning Marcel to London to wave her hair and paying him the princely sum of two thousand francs, an unprecedented fee for a mere hairdresser. In fact the massive revenue enjoyed by Marcel was one of the reasons why he became such a hero to the British trade, so much so that in 1908 he was lured to London for a forty-five minute demonstration advertised as the Fête

Fête Marcel, 1908

A HAIRDRESSERS' COMPETITION : SKETCHES AT THE "CONCOURS INTERNATIONAL" AT THE CAFE MONICO, LONDON.
Republished by permission of the Proprietors of "THE DAILY GRAPHIC."

**Students practising
Marcel-waving on
blocks, 1930s**

Marcel, and as this was the first time Marcel had demonstrated his technique in public the event was a major publicity draw. After a day's sightseeing in a brake, visiting such London landmarks as the Albert Memorial, Regent's Park Zoo and the Tower of London, Marcel and his London patron, Boudu, held hairdressers spellbound with 'the most remarkable gathering that the hairdressing trade has ever witnessed'.[1] Heating his irons over a gas burner, Marcel cut and waved a model's hair, basked in the applause and then repaired to the ballroom for a night's dancing. Accolade piled on accolade after the prestigious event. One enraptured hairdresser wrote, 'We cannot remember any hairdresser, in all the Trade archives, who ever hit upon a fashion in hair which ever secured a thousandth part of the universality which is accorded to the Marcel wave', and added rather tellingly, 'Or, again, we cannot recall any fashion or device in

[1] HAIRDRESSERS' WEEKLY JOURNAL, 1 August 1908, p.1143

hair which has ever produced so much revenue and continuous revenue to hairdressers as the Marcel wave. Further, was there ever a hairdresser prior to Monsieur Marcel who had such a prolific patronage that lady clients of wealth and social distinction formed a long and eager queue, awaiting their "turn" for his services like out-patients at a hospital or "first nighters" at a theatre, and even taking precedence by purchasing the top positions in the queue.'[1] By 1917 Emile Long recognized that the Marcel wave had become the rage throughout all strata of British society, so that 'now there is not even a modest work-girl or shop assistant who does not resort to its infinite possibilities'.[2]

[1] Ibid.

[2] HAIRDRESSERS' WEEKLY JOURNAL, March 1917

A hairdresser who could Marcel-wave was eagerly sought out by women and queues would form daily in the street and up the stairs of salons for an appointment with a hairdresser trained in its effects. The technique became such a staple of the hairdresser's craft that it was in use until the end of the 1930s and was still being taught to hairdressing students in the 1960s to provide a good basic training for imparting a 'feeling' for the structure of hair. Students practised on wefts of hair pinned firmly to blocks, old felt hats which were stuffed for the purpose or even the corner of a settee at home, and a poorly trained hairdresser could be easily spotted. Hanckel told novices in 1937, 'It requires long and arduous hours of practice. It is an art in itself and requires much care and precision and an eye for beauty to achieve results which go to the making of a perfect picture.'[3] The use of the word 'art' was important as the Marcel wave was one of the practices to distinguish between the ladies' hairdresser and the barber and an insensitive practitioner in its effects was regarded as a philistine incapable of making the correct

[3] Hanckel, p.22

aesthetic judgements. The Parisian hairdresser Antoine was one amongst many who cautioned women to beware of 'old Marcels' which 'resembled the general lines of the rougher part of a washboard',[1] for an indelicate coiffeur could produce deep, coarse waves that made a natural head of hair resemble a cheap wig. In fact the bad Marcel became a style associated with a rather tarty type of woman, a look which Hanckel snootily remarked was 'practically unknown in the West End, but is more in evidence among a certain type of the working class'.[2]

[1] Antoine, p.158

[2] Hanckel p.23

Just two years before the Fête came the breakthrough which was to lead to the end of the Marcel wave. The news of the invention of a permanent curl came on 22 September 1906 when the *Hairdressers' Weekly Journal* announced an invitation from Mr C. Nestlé of 245 Oxford Street, W1, who 'begs to invite leading hairdressers to inspect and judge a lady's hair waved permanently by his newly invented and greatly improved process of waving to withstand water, shampoo and all atmospheric influences. Every investigation allowed.' Further demonstrations were carried out throughout the following years during which Nestlé wound the model's hair around metal curlers and then covered it with small lengths of bandage impregnated with a special solution. The *Hairdressers' Weekly Journal* described the new process in 1909 where a woman's hair was 'encased in asbestos and baked for ten minutes by means of a specially and ingeniously devised electrical heater hanging from a well-conceived bracket in such a manner as to take all the weight from the head. Each of the heaters — and there are a number — require as much electricity as an eight-candle power lamp. A double layer of brown paper was placed near the head to keep as much heat from the head as possible, and an assistant with a small bellows was kept occupied for a similar purpose. At the completion of the work the hair was shampooed, and was shown after drying to have retained its frizziness.'[1] This was the very first practical salon permanent wave, invented by Karl Ludwig Nessler, born in Todtnau, Germany, in 1872.

[1] HAIRDRESSERS' WEEKLY JOURNAL, 13 March 1909, p. 435

Nessler had initially been apprenticed to a barber in his local village and after moving to Switzerland took up hairdressing, anglicized his name to Charles Nestlé and began experimenting on hair with various gadgets, trying to come up with a method of producing a permanent wave. In 1901 he moved to London and worked as a hairdresser in Leicester Square but was sacked when discovered trying out his own inventions on one of the clients instead of Marcel-waving. Despite this setback, by 1902 Nestlé had opened his own London salon in Great Castle Street, where permanent waves were regularly produced by one enormous overhead machine hanging from the ceiling like some weird chandelier, made up of heavy heaters, brass curlers and borax rods balanced by weights. The first brave clients had their hair suffused with chemicals, wound round the curlers, which were covered up with borax tubes and the whole thing heated by electrical current. Women who were prepared to give the new process a go found themselves stuck under an extremely weighty mechanical contraption for hours at a time, looking and probably feeling as if they were undergoing some particularly nasty form of futuristic torture. The chemical reaction caused by the heating eventually made the sulphur bonds holding the hair break, to re-form around the curlers and, after the

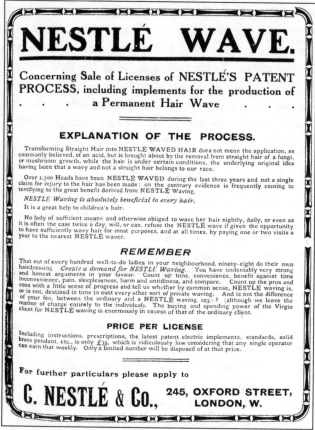

NESTLÉ WAVE.

Concerning Sale of Licenses of NESTLÉ'S PATENT PROCESS, including implements for the production of . . . a Permanent Hair Wave . . .

EXPLANATION OF THE PROCESS.

Transforming Straight Hair into NESTLÉ WAVED HAIR does not mean the application, as commonly believed, of an acid, but is brought about by the removal from straight hair of a fungi, or mushroom growth, while the hair is under certain conditions, the underlying original idea having been that a wavy and not a straight hair belongs to our race.

Over 1,700 Heads have been NESTLÉ WAVED during the last three years and not a single claim for injury to the hair has been made; on the contrary evidence is frequently coming in testifying to the great benefit derived from NESTLÉ Waving.

NESTLÉ Waving is absolutely beneficial to every hair.

It is a great help to children's hair.

No lady of sufficient means and otherwise obliged to wave her hair nightly, daily, or even as it is often the case twice a day, will, or can. refuse the NESTLÉ wave if given the opportunity to have sufficiently wavy hair for most purposes, and at all times, by paying one or two visits a year to the nearest NESTLÉ waver.

REMEMBER

That out of every hundred well-to-do ladies in your neighbourhood, ninety-eight do their own hairdressing *Create a demand for NESTLÉ Waving.* You have undeniably very strong and honest arguments in your favour. Count up time, convenience, benefit against time inconvenience, pain, sleeplessness, harm and untidiness, and compare. Count up the pros and cons with a little sense of progress and tell us whether by common sense, NESTLÉ waving is, or is not, destined in time to oust every other sort of private waving. And is not the difference of your fee, between the ordinary and a NESTLÉ waving. 103/-? (although we leave the matter of charge entirely to the individual). The buying and spending power of the Virgin client for NESTLÉ waving is enormously in excess of that of the ordinary client.

PRICE PER LICENSE

Including instructions, prescriptions, the latest patent electric implements, standards, solid brass pendant, etc., is only £35, which is ridiculously low considering that any single operator can earn that weekly. Only a limited number will be disposed of at that price.

For further particulars please apply to

C. NESTLÉ & Co., 245, OXFORD STREET, LONDON, W.

application of a neutralizer, be permanently retained in a new curly form. Hard-wearing curls were created because the internal structure of the hair had been fundamentally changed.

The process wasn't without its problems, though. Even after the very first demonstrations in the early 1900s complaints had been made and Nestlé had to mount a counter-offensive in the pages of the *Hairdressers' Weekly*

Journal after one of his models' head showed 'two inflamed spots, which became painful, and developed a septic ulcer, which necessitated the young girl's detention in her room for five weeks, and leaving consequently a bald spot near the crown of her head the size of a six penny piece or smaller'.[1]

A series of advertisements in 1911 tried to convince the trade that 'the Nestlé wave of today is more than that of 1906. It is something like the difference between the modern coupé and the ancient boneshaker of 1901. Nestlé-waving was then, with

[1] HAIRDRESSERS' WEEKLY JOURNAL, 29 January 1910, p.186

Advertisement for the Nestlé's permanent hairwave, 1911

NESTLE'S PERMANENT HAIRWAVE

(Concerning our offer to give 50 Licenses, Apparatus, Implements, Instructions and Prescriptions on approval, JOURNAL, Oct. 28th).

A Child's Nestle-waved Hair.

The same head before it was waved.

C. NESTLE & CO., 48, South Molton Street, LONDON, W.

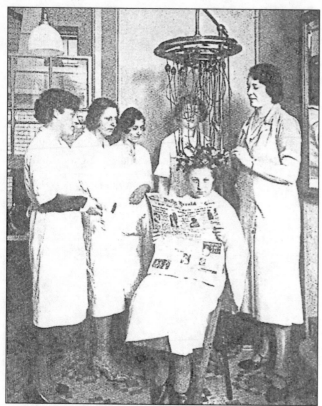

Students being instructed in permanent waving, 1930s

some justification, called "frizz making". There were clients and there would have been a hundred times more had our trade never been alienated with benzine and tetra-chloride of carbon. In an average of from 50 to 60 letters which we receive daily, the interest of the feminine public in this discovery is evident, but what is still more striking is the fear of death which beholds the public. Is there any fear of death in the Nestlé process?' The advertisement made it clear that there was not.

Despite Nestlé's protestations to the contary, injuries during the perming process were fairly commonplace as the chemical solutions involved had to be heated to above two hundred degrees and burning the scalp was a distinct possibility. To prevent possible mishaps, safety items such as spacers of felt were placed strategically between the electric curlers and the client's head, but the porcelain rods frequently overheated, melting their Bakelite cores, and some women faced the painful indignity of having a head full of melted plastic. Electric shocks were also a regular occurrence. As late as 1931 Foan was advising hairdressers of the emergency procedures to employ if electrocution seemed severe, telling the employer to keep the patient warm, with the head low and 'hot weak brandy and water should be administered every few minutes, about a teaspoonful at a time'.[1] Even if the client managed to avoid these perils many inexperienced perm operators tended to overheat the hair, loosening its cuticle cells and making it dry, brittle and liable to break off, or made the hair too curly so it had to be hidden away under a scarf to avoid ridicule. From the 1930s these varied effects made the use of setting lotions popular: concoctions used to moisten the hair before and after the perming event, usually made up of alkalis and borax or gum substances in spirit and water, liberally scented to disguise the rather chemical smell. Some women created their own setting lotions at home from beaten egg and water and sometimes even applied olive oil directly onto their hair. Unfortunately, however much care was taken, there were always some women who left the salon with less money, less hair and a singed head.

[1] Foan, p.327

147

The original Nestlé perms were an endurance test as they could take up to ten hours if the client wanted her whole head curled and used over three or four separate processes. They were also very expensive because of the arduousness of the task involved and the fact that there were very few salons in which the curling could take place. Despite this, the perm was nothing short of a miracle for women who wanted waves which lasted for months and defied washing, and its popularity led to many a bizarre experiment by hairdressers wanting to cash in on the new craze. Raymond remembered the boss of a salon called Maison Rigi of Victoria attempting his own system of wet-curling: 'Since he could not very well practise on his clients he decided that I should be the guinea pig as I was the junior in the salon. Foolishly I agreed to take part in the experiment. He wound my hair – it was quite long – round a collection of metal rods, which each had a French letter filled with a fluid of his concoction attached to the base. Clipped to each contraption was an element. The idea was that the power conducted through the French letter would heat the rods and thus curl the hair. What in fact happened was that the liquid in the French letters boiled and they exploded and I was scalded.'[1]

P.K. Sartory, inventor of 'Superma'

[1] Raymond, p.43

More successful modifications were made to Nestlé's machine by various inventors, including Eugene Suter, who introduced a perforated sachet and two-way curler under the name of 'Eugene', and the MacDonald brothers, who invented the kettle system of waving whereby a permanent curl was produced using pure steam. However, these techniques still used the chandelier. It was not until Peter Sartory produced a chemical pad which created its own heat after immersion in water and did away with having to sit under the perming

Permanent-waving by machine, c. 1920s

machine for hours on end that women were liberated from the 'octopus'. In Sartory's technique the same chemical reagent was used on the hair, the hair wound around a spiral curler and then the pad applied, producing permanent waves quickly by a combination of lotion and heat from the pad — a less taxing and more controlled experience than the machine perm. Exothermic pads were marketed very successfully under the name 'Superma', solving 'the problem of the woman who is afraid of machinery', and became especially popular during the Second World War because of the shortages in materials and the restrictions in the use of electricity.

The first single solution cold wave to be successfully patented was developed by Professor Speakman of Leeds University in 1936, a far simpler process which eliminated all extraneous hardware, but it was only after the war that this product was available in Britain when the chemicals required could be manufactured to meet demand. Speakman's method is still the accepted system of producing a perm.

Bob before and after a perm, 1922

Permed and shingled hairstyles, c. 1930s

The perm really took off in the 1930s when used in conjunction with the shorter, easier-to-care-for bob. A softer, tousled, more traditionally feminine look using curls and fringes was imported from Paris. Dubbed the 'floue' or 'Qua Neglige', it used the techniques of Antoine's sculptured curl and was made available to women thanks to the new perming technology. These fashionable longer variations on the bob had many evocative names, such as the Windblown

151

of 1932, Cherub, Cringle and the Madonna; they shared a fullness in the back of the hair as well as the front, unlike the styles of the 1920s. To create these looks more and more women wanted access to the new perming and setting techniques available at the hairdresser's and business boomed. As the fashionable look of the day also demanded a neat, bandbox appearance, the exciting new perm was seen as the modern way to tame unruly hair, so preventing 'tonsorial chaos', particularly for the woman who was becoming more and more interested in sport, fitness and exercise. In magazines and beauty books of the day women were cautioned against 'uncontrolled' locks and in 1935 Agnes Savill was one of the first to applaud the perm's efficacy on 'wet and blustering days [when] there were too often seen thin, unkempt strands of hair straying untidily over the brows, ears and neck. In the damp, windy climate of Britain, the permanent wave is useful for preserving a tidy coiffure.'[1]

[1] Savill, p.56

Not all women could afford the new process, however. Raymond remembered customers so poor they 'could not afford any luxury treatments, not even a shampoo. We would have to curl and crimp with curling tongs, and the smell from the greasy, dirty hair when the hot tongs were applied was overpowering.'[2] Those who could afford the perm also had to be advised on how to look after it properly. After the initial expense many women tended to steer away from brushing and combing lest they ruined the effect of the waves and Savill described 'factory workers' who so irregularly brushed their hair 'that pediculosis has become prevalent amongst them'.[3] Clear advice began to be given on how best to care for the new waves in women's magazines and beauty books of the day, and women were told to brush

[2] Raymond, pp.41–2

[3] Savill, p.60

Edwardian postcard, c. 1900s

Sing a Song of Sixpence,
A bottle full of dye,
Four and twenty grey hairs
Touched up by and by.

and comb their hair thoroughly each evening before bed and then give their scalps a few minutes' finger massage. The waves were then pushed back into position and eau-de-Cologne sprinkled over the head. There were also criticisms of the perm from those who believed the process had sounded the death knell for individuality in women's hairstyling. For one critic:

'As regards the aesthetic value of the permanent wave, few modern hairdressers have any skill in deciding the form of wave suitable for the individual client. As the average modern woman also has a low artistic standard, she is ignorant about the style of hairdressing which would bring out the best points of her features. The popular, perfectly set and oiled coiffure has its own undoubted attraction, but those who love beauty have grown to dislike the sameness of the neatly arranged heads so transparently prepared for formal functions and for the public eye. The thousands of these identically regular and obviously machine-made waves are the despair of artists, who wish to paint portraits of individual women, no two of whom has nature created on the same plane.'[1]

[1] Savill, p.60

Advertisements for hairdyes, c. 1900s and 1920

This compulsion to curl in the 1930s was not to be outdone by women's recourse to the dye bottle and attitudes to the practices of dyeing and bleaching changed dramatically in the twentieth century. Victorian women had dyed their hair, disguising greyness with peculiar mixtures of balsam, sulphur, lead, beef marrow and castor oil, then setting it with lotions of carbonate of potassium, glycerine, ammonia, spirit and rosewater. The earliest dyes were natural extracts like henna, which was used in salons up to the late 1930s. The finely ground root of the henna plant was mixed with water into a thick paste, brought to the boil in a double saucepan and then applied to the client's hair, having first smeared her forehead and the tips of her ears with Vaseline to prevent the skin from being stained. The client's head was then wrapped in brown paper for thirty minutes to an hour, depending on the depth of colour required. Camomile powder was also in general use to brighten blondeness.

In 1909 the first carefully marketed range of hair dyes was offered commercially to the public under the name of L'Oréal, invented by the chemist Eugène Schueller, although chemical dyes had been in use in the the Parisian salons of Monnet et Cie since 1883. These original dyes were para-compounds of para-phenylene diamine or para-toluylene, a derivative of coal tar which when mixed with a small amount of peroxide produced a variety of shades from auburn to black which were permanent. Dye books had to be kept for individual clients so the exact shades could be matched up, an art which had to be carried out by a hairdresser rather than the woman 'touching up' at home. Even then hairdressers could make mistakes. One who had done so and feared legal action described his problem to the legal advisers Messrs Plunkett and Leader in 1904, signing his letter 'Anxious': 'I have used a dye made in Paris. The lady had bleached her hair with peroxide. When she came her hair was dark at the roots, the ends light blonde, and the outside very much bleached. I applied the dye, which I consider quite harmless, but the hair became redder than we expected. After several shampoos and more peroxide, I made it lighter, but she was not satisfied and returned with a specialist, who asked to know the preparation I used. The lady would not allow me to finish, and naturally I have been unable to complete my work and remove the preparation. She thinks I should destroy her hair. I fear she may take proceedings against me. What is the best course to take in a legal way?' The advice was grim: 'There is nothing for you to do, as far as we can see; if you have been negligent in your treatment you will be liable in damages.'[1]

Hair dyeing dangers, 1914

Problems kept recurring, for although these dyes had the required effect colour-wise, they were notoriously toxic. Early experiments on a dog had turned its blood black and it had expired shortly afterwards. In 1931 the author of THE ART AND CRAFT OF LADIES' HAIRDRESSING felt compelled to describe the allergic reactions to look out for in clients undergoing treatments in the salon: 'First of all there appear small pimples, or pustules, and these are accompanied by intolerable itchings, followed by a kind of eczema; the skin is violet red, inflamed, damp and oozing; there are swellings underneath the eye and the eyelids — the eyes themselves may also be affected, so that the patient is unable to open them — and frequently the entire face is swollen. The forehead is often burnt and blistered,

Advertisement for hair dye, 1920

JANUARY 31, 1920.   THE HAIRDRESSERS' WEEKLY JOURNAL   209

Coiffeur de Dames   Maison Ace

"That's That!" says the lady who has had her hair treated with

INECTO RAPID

for she understands that as far as the restored colour of her hair is concerned she is SATISFIED FOR LIFE -

Sole Selling Agents—
OSBORNE, GARRETT and COMPANY, LIMITED
LONDON and BIRMINGHAM

and the neck is covered with red patches. The lips are red and thick, and sometimes the complete interior of the mouth is swollen, ulceration supervening. Violent headaches and shivering are also felt, and, in chronic cases, the legs and feet become swollen.'[1] After several reported cases of rashes and fever, one directly related death from pneumonia and the successful suing of the manufacturers of one brand of dye in 1922, Germany banned the use of para-dyes. Britain responded with one of the first instances of consumer protection in the 1933 Pharmacy and Poison Act, which made warnings on packaging and a patch test a legal requirement in any salon. Gilbert Foan also sounded a warning to hairdressers in the same year: 'A number of hairdressers have been involved in legal costs, and in some cases additional heavy damages have been awarded to clients who have become poisoned by a hair dye application. So serious have been some of the cases that many insurance companies now refuse to cover a hairdresser against what is known as "hair dye risks".'[2] There was also the problem of women not having much of a clue about which colours actually suited them: the mutton dressed as lamb brigade, who seemed to be particularly attracted to the youthful effects of the dye bottle no matter what the consequences. Hanckel told of 'an elderly client of eighty-three' who had come to him in great concern: 'She possessed a scanty head of hair, extremely thin, and jet black in colour, which she informed me had been wrongly treated, and instead of the Clara Bow titian hue, which she so ardently wished to obtain, a head of black hair had resulted. She was most anxious to have the dye removed and the lighter colour introduced.'[3]

For most of the 1930s, however, one of the most popular

[1] Foan, p.365

[2] Ibid. p.364

[3] Hanckel, p.37

changes of hair colour was from mousy or dark to blonde, the Jean Harlow as opposed to Clara Bow look. Hydrogen peroxide was originally invented by the chemist Thénard in 1818, but it wasn't until much later in the next century that its cosmetic potential was realized. In 1901 *Queen* magazine was still insisting, 'It is absurd to think that any hair on the head can be bleached. It is said to have been done by Americans in America and in Paris, but though we have devoted a good deal of time both in New York and in the French capital to ascertain how this can be done, we have never been able to discover anybody who will ...'[1] But by the 1930s the real fashion for blondeness as an artificial as opposed to natural look came in. The success of blonder than blonde film stars like Jean Harlow promoted an extreme version of the fashion in films like *Platinum Blonde* of 1931, where her lurid phosphorescent locks kickstarted the obsession which exists today with stars such as Pamela Anderson. Women had their hair bleached in imitation of Harlow and by 1932 sales of peroxide had zoomed, up by 35 per cent in America alone. To achieve the platinum effect hairdressers used a rinse of methylene blue or diluted methyl violet, creating a whiter than white appearance by taking out the notorious yellow tinge. Irving Schulman lyrically and rather unquestioningly described the longevity of the look over thirty years later in 1964, seeing Jean Harlow as the woman who 'typified the distinctive, unique type of American beauty, which has since been imitated throughout the world. Succeeding decades have modified that beauty, but basically it is gay, carefree, healthy and athletic, wholesomely sexual without being furtive and dirty: and always it is blonde.'[2] This type of American beauty was not available to all, however, and Richard Dyer has commented on how this

[1] Corson, p.602

[2] Irving Schulman, HARLOW: AN INTIMATE BIOGRAPHY, (London, Mayflower, 1962), p. 352

particular brand of high-status glamour reflects the values of the dominant group, the white American. He sees a sinister aspect to this supposedly wholesome look which forms part of the whole worship of Aryan culture which was so prevalent in the 1930s and ultimately involved the Nazi project. This was a hair-style limited to white women, an exclusionary look of segregation being promoted at exactly the same time as the growing respectability and thus acceptance of the National Association for the Advancement of Colored People and the corresponding backlash in the rapid expansion in membership of the Ku Klux Klan. Thus the platinum blonde of 1930s Hollywood reinforced the hysteria hiding behind the supposedly unbiased promotion of a hair colour which was in actuality singling out and proposing a superior racial stock.

In the 1930s as more and more women succumbed to the peroxide bottle, blondeness began to lose its high status and the disparaging term 'bottle blonde' began to be used. Cheap hair bleaching with thinly disguised black roots began to be associated with the 'easy' working-class woman. As one man was prepared to admit, 'To me a blonde means good times and better sex.'[1] Women were advised to think carefully before embarking on such a dramatic change, however. One beauty writer warned, 'Think well before you decide to bleach or dye, because once started, it takes time and money to continue the practice. Even in the midst of illness, it will be necessary to keep up the deception if you hope to safeguard your beauty secret. Most men abhor the artificiality of bleached or dyed hair, and you must be very sure of the advisability of such a procedure before you ever start. Nature is too fine a cosmetician to have gotten mixed up in the colour harmony she created for you when you were

[1] Schulman, p.11

born. I think most women look younger and prettier when they let nature decide about the colour of their hair. Bleached hair becomes too brassy and metallic to fool anyone, no matter how skillfully the work is done.'[1] Even Harlow had to conform and, if asked, explained that her hair colour was natural due to the bleaching effects of the sun. When pressed by the Hollywood agent Arthur Landau, she admitted to putting a 'little blueing' in the water when she washed her hair.

[1] Veronica Dengel, CAN I HOLD MY BEAUTY?, (London, John Westhouse Publishers Ltd, 1946), p. 30

Bleaching was also believed to be dangerous to the health. Harlow's early demise at the age of twenty-six was rumoured to be the result of the repeated use of peroxide and the absorption of the toxic chemicals through her scalp had supposedly destroyed her kidneys. Her rabid interest in such superficialities as hair-dos had apparently killed her and this fatal obsession with fashion exemplified the cautionary tale of patriarchy — that all women have to tread a thin line between being suitably alluring and quite literally a fashion victim. So, with blondeness a little bit of lightening was considered acceptable but too much and a woman risked appearing a bit 'fast', lower class, a sporter of an artificial disguise that was unnatural and cheating, misrepresenting age or 'natural' beauty. In fact considering whether to bleach, dye or tint was such a sensitive issue that the practice was not openly referred to until the 1950s and women used the code word 'treatment' instead.

Trainee hairdressers were advised: 'Read all you can about hair colouring. Update your vocabulary. Discard the word "dye", say "tint" instead. Avoid such harsh, frightening words as "stripping". In place of the word "bleach" use the word "lighten".'[2]

[2] Miriam Cordwell and Marion Rudoy, HAIR DESIGN AND FASHION: PRINCIPLES AND RELATIONSHIPS, (New York, Crown Publishers Inc, 1956), p.9

The popularity of blondeness soared in the 1950s

Blondeness enjoyed a second surge of popularity in the 1950s amongst young women who wanted to emulate Hollywood stars Grace Kelly, Kim Novak and the giggling Marilyn Monroe with her conflation of blonde glamour with stupidity, childhood innocence and sexual abandon. This ideal state of sexualized, socialized womanhood was exemplified by the launch of Barbie as a blonde, following the tradition of girlhood icons having long golden hair. Little girls had always been persuaded that princesses looked this way and now they had a contemporary icon to reinforce this mythology.

'Cool' blondeness in the 1950s

To go blonde meant undergoing rather basic treatments. Vidal Sassoon remembered making 'diabolical bleaches, mixing twenty-volume peroxide in a bowl with three drops of ammonia. I had to add the drops, the number had to be exact; and I was terrified my hand would shake — it was as primitive as that.'[1] However, women were prepared to risk the

[1]Trasko, Georgina Howell, 'The Big Shear', in AMERICAN VOGUE, (January 1993, p. 84)

The brunette, 1960

ruination of their hair because of the dramatic changes bleaching wrought, for the blonde myth meant more than just being beautiful. The beauty writer Lois Wyse made this clear: 'Without blonde, a woman can be just another pretty face, and pretty faces are a dime a dozen. Brunettes wear boots all year round: blondes wear strappy sandals.'[1] Blonde was not just a look, it was a whole psychology, clearly identified in one of the most successful advertising campaigns in haircare history. 'If I have only one life to live: let me live it as a blonde' went the catchphrase created by the copywriter

[1] Lois Wyse, BLONDE BEAUTIFUL BLONDE: HOW TO LOOK, LIVE, WORK AND THINK BLONDE, (New York, Mary Evans and Co, 1980), p.159

Shirley Polykoff to launch the Clairol home-dyeing kits, which made hair colouring cheaper, easier and domesticated. Clairol's products just needed to be applied once, with lightener and toner together, and even though the underlying appeal of the advertising campaign was obviously sexualized — 'Does she or doesn't she? Only her hairdresser knows for sure' — attitudes were definitely changing. In the 1940s dye discoveries were made at an even more rapid pace. In 1946 Clairol marketed semi-permanent colour rinses for brightening 'mousy' hair which were marketed for the use of young women, a completely new concept as formerly dyes were directed at the older woman who wanted to disguise her greying hair. Changing hair colour was now fun and fashionable and the effect of the colour coating the hair shafts could last up to six weeks. By the 1950s dyes originally used in the fur industry were found to be suitable for hair, making a whole new range of shades possible from chestnut, auburn and burgundy red through to blue black. They were safer than para-dyes and easy enough in their application to be used at home; despite a slight hitch in 1955, when a shipment of 'Natural Brown' from Germany had the unfortunate effect of turning hair a becoming shade of bright green, the new dyes were very successful. Raymond was one of the first hairdressers of any repute to get in on the act, turning hair ash blonde by first bleaching, then colouring it with very strong coffee or tea, finally adding two drops of oil of cloves to the mixture to conceal the peculiar smell.

By the 1950s bleaching and dyeing the hair was on its way to becoming respectable. To illustrate this sea change of opinion, as early as 1954 beauty writer Betty Page said, 'It is no longer "arty" or in doubtful taste to change the colour of

Semi-permanent hair rinses in the late 1950s

your hair',[1] and another commentator described how 'a few years ago, women would tint their hair only if it were greying, either normally or prematurely. The requirements were simple, and mostly carried out in a cubicle — almost under a cloak of secrecy. Though the work is still carried out to a large degree in privacy, women no longer feel they must be apologetic when asking for a tint. Younger women accept naturally and use it in various ways, and older people are shedding their inhibitions.'[2]

[1] Betty Page, ON FAIR VANITY (London, Convoy Publications Ltd, 1954), p.163

[2] Charles Revson in Grant McCracken, BIG HAIR: A JOURNEY INTO THE TRANSFORMATION OF SELF, (London, Penguin, 1995), p.96

Blonde, brunette or redhead? The respectability of hair dyeing in late 1950s

One obvious factor for this embracing of new products was the joy in their availability after years of wartime austerity. Women's hair had suffered during the Second World War. Perms had been out of the question because of the restrictions in the manufacture of chemicals, some of which were used to make munitions and diverted for the war effort. Women were not to be put off and resorted to a ragbag of methods to achieve a curl, even such uncomfortable and sticky ones as putting a mixture of sugar and water on the hair, curling it with pipe cleaners and leaving it overnight. Throughout the 1940s it was very difficult for women to have their hair done professionally unless they had a bit of spare cash and could afford to go to places like the basement bomb-shelter salon at the Dorchester Hotel, so fashions were severely limited and for the most part hair-styles were not that amazingly different from those of the 1930s. There were the odd homages to the war-worker woman with the fashion for devices such as glamour bands and scarves twisted around the head and tied in a roll at the front, used to keep hair neat at the munitions factory and to hide the shortages of soap and hairdressers. When the war ended this headgear became the stereotype of the charlady or working-class wife like Hilda Ogden in the seminal soap opera *Coronation Street.* The Hollywood fashion for a peek-a-boo fringe inspired by Veronica Lake was not particularly popular in Britain, and it supposedly led to horrific accidents when women's hair was caught in machinery. The most prevalent vogue was for sausage-shaped curls rolled in a row along the forehead with the back caught up with pins in the classic Betty Grable style or left to flow over the shoulders, although by 1954 Betty Page was counselling women against this style: 'You may look attractive seated in front of a mirror with your hair hanging about your shoulders [but] when you stand up you turn into a witch' and 'Older women are a bit ridiculous with long manes on their shoulders, or too many curls.'[1]

[1] Page, p.34

The condition of women's hair was not helped by the overuse of inferior home perms and the extravagant wielding of curling tongs. Hair had been one of the only parts of the appearance that was unrationed so rather high, rolled hair-dos were the style of the times. At the end of the war women flocked to the salon to have a professional perm for the first time in years, but as the 1950s wore on, home perms became more sophisticated and thus more popular. The Toni-Gillette Company and the Toni perm began to dominate the market, with the catchphrase 'Which twin has the Toni?' making perming a more common domestic event, even though beauty writers such as Constance Moore located the home perm within working-class culture, the preserve of the rather lowly drudge. The go-getting woman who *really* cared went to the salon; she was the 'business women to whom "time is money" and who wanted – and can afford – the very highest standard of appearance'.[1] Perming was a new indoor sport, perfect in the era of the Happy Housewife when all sorts of domestic goddesses from mothers and daughters to sisters and girlfriends could be happily ensconced at home of an evening, surrounded by jugs, wet end-papers, curlers, and the pungent smell of thioglycollic acid. Accordingly hundreds of beauty books were published counselling women on how to achieve the fashionable ideal, and a strict style policy, determined by developments in French haute couture with the correct accompanying hair-styles, cosmetics and accessories, had to be followed if one wanted to appear 'well turned out'. To follow all this advice successfully, women were supposed to embark on time-consuming beauty routines, for this was the era of advice for the young housewife, mother and ageing woman who had to be on guard at all times to prevent the attentions of her wayward husband straying.

[1] Constance Moore, THE WAY TO BEAUTY, (London, Ward, Lock and Co. Ltd, 1955), pp.35–6

**Beauty routines of the
1950s**

Some beauty procedures were still rather rudimentary in the early 1950s — one popular method of dealing with the problem of dry hair was to steep it in castor oil and hot water before shampooing and home-made shampoos of shredded Knight's Castile soap and water simmered in a saucepan were not unusual — but the technological advances stemming from the Second World War had enormous effects on the hair industry. The shortage of fats to make soap, for instance, led

to the development of synthetic detergents. This meant that the first soapless shampoos became available which removed the problems of getting soap scum off the hair with lemon rinses. The 1950s consumer could buy any number of varieties by companies such as French of London, Boots and Bristow and many of the new shampoos contained lanolin, considered an enriching nourishment for the scalp. In between shampoos women were encouraged to use an oil conditioning dressing in cream or oil, the most popular brands being Vitapoint or Countess. It was also still possible to dry-shampoo the hair between washes, a practice which had been very popular from the late nineteenth century to the 1970s. The main reason for its use in the 1950s was the palaver that getting a bowl of hot water entailed in many

Advert for Silvikrin shampoo, 1960, advising women to 'wash hair every seven days'

houses, but there was also the taboo about washing the hair during menstruation, as it was believed to be harmful for women to be in contact with too much water when the body was in a weakened state. The dry shampoos of the 1950s involved the use of basic Robin household starch or orris root. Partings were made in the hair, the starch dabbed on until it was evenly white all over, left for ten minutes to absorb the grease, and then the hair was brushed to remove all traces; occasionally eau-de-Cologne or white spirit was used to the same effect. Eventually the practice of dry-shampooing died out due to the increasing availability of hair-dryers and constant hot water in many homes.

The relationship between diet and hair condition was almost obsessional during this decade, a precursor to attitudes in the 1980s and 1990s. Constance Moore in THE WAY TO BEAUTY advised women: 'Pay attention to your diet if dry hair persists. It may well be that you are not getting enough fat in your food: a little extra butter, dripping, cream, a few foods cooked in olive oil or with margarine, may make all the difference to the condition of your skin and scalp.'[1] Oily hair was sometimes attributed to the eating of too much pork, pepper and pickles. Sufferers were also cautioned against headscarves and tight-fitting hats and told to rub salt into their scalp before shampooing, a curious throwback to the nineteenth century. Perhaps the most bizarre relationship between hair and health was the complete fixation in the 1950s with bowel movements, as the cure for most hair ills was believed to be 'regularity'. Veronica Dengel in CAN I HOLD MY BEAUTY? had this stark advice for women:

[1] Moore, p.31

'Unless you establish a regular schedule of bowel elimination, you cannot hope to have shiny hair. Retention of body waste in the large colon is a certain method of ruining your health, youth and beauty. Failure to respond to the physical urge for a bowel movement is one of the greatest and gravest causes of constipation among civilized peoples. If you have the slightest inclination, obey it. An effort should be made each morning. Choose a time when you can relax quietly. Plan to sit on the toilet for at least ten minutes unless an elimination is accomplished sooner. It is helpful to rest the feet on a little footstool, and bend forward so as to compress the abdomen against the thighs, duplicating the squatting position of primitive man. Make an effort to be quietly relaxed – don't let your mind rush off in disturbing thoughts about how much you have to do today. Read, or even inspect your eyebrows for attention; or file your nails. But stay there!'[1]

[1] Dengel, p.106

Dandruff was also a major worry, viewed as 'a splendid vehicle for carrying germs and infections of the scalp, which is why trying on hats, using other people's combs and brushes, or leaning back unprotected in railway carriages can be a risky procedure'.[2] To eradicate the problem one had to use a medicated scurf lotion containing sulphur such as Pragmatur and using some of the new conditioning products helped. By the early 1950s, different solutions were available for different types of hair, some quite peculiar by modern standards, and instead of jojoba or oil of evening primrose, placenta, oil of mink and wheat germ were available, some of the mixtures changing very little until the early 1970s.

[2] Moore, p.32

A good cut was considered essential, the basic foundation of a complex styling process, and as all 'modern' hair-styles

All sorts of exciting and enchanting things to do with your hair

Pins and rollers

involved perming, shaping or cutting the hair every five to six weeks and then setting, hairdressers were doing very well. Hair had to be set professionally into a *pli* at least once a week and then 'dressed out' in the salon using a nylon brush. Women who couldn't afford such regular excursions to the hairdresser's set their hair at home and gave it extra 'body' with grips as rollers were still rather expensive. As in the nineteenth century, brushes and brushing were an important part of a woman's beauty routine and used to bring the hair's natural oil from the root to the ends and give a shine. It was still the orthodoxy to wash hair rather infrequently, just dampening and setting it into pin curls at home and then

'Sexual play' in beauty routines, c. 1950s

Drier

[1] Anon., MODERN LIVING: YOUR LOOKS, (LONDON, 1963), p.69

[2] Ibid., p.21

tweaking it into the same rigid style every morning, but this popular method had serious effects on the scalp, making it as 'dry and arid as the Sahara',[1] so brushing was stressed by many beauty writers in an attempt to overcome the problem by breaking up the accumulated residues of dirt and sebum. By 1963 brushing techniques were still being advocated in MODERN LIVING: YOUR LOOKS:[2] the right result could be obtained by 'long, root-to-tip strokes for four minutes by the clock every evening [to] give results which, if they could only be bottled, would have rich women standing in long queues to pay

**Feminine
seductiveness in
beauty routines,
c. 1950s**

guineas for them!' Bristle brushes were recommended for home use and nylon brushes were not to be used there under any circumstances for fear of 'scraping' the scalp. Here women could indulge themselves, as brushing the hair still had the sexualized overtones of the nineteenth century, although the hair-styles in the 1950s were considerably shorter and there wasn't that much to let down. This was a beauty activity which could form a part of sexual play between a happily married couple and Dengel explained in rapt tones, 'You can make a lovely picture in your bedroom if you sit in the soft light and wear a becoming negligee. Brush thoroughly, but gracefully, keeping each movement consciously beautiful. Perhaps you will need a little private practice, but when you are fairly proficient, try the effect on your husband. Watch an actress next time she is shown brushing her hair. The frequency with which this bit is injected into pictures about married life proves it is a calculated effect for creating glamour.'[1] The art of brushing was also one of the most important elements of a student's training. Foan in

[1] Dengel, p.31

Six styles from one set, c. 1950s

**L: 'City Style'
R: 'Tomboy'**

**L: '1930s'
R: 'Young Idea'**

**L: 'Mary Tudor'
R: 'Country Casual'**

particular thought a standardized system should be taught as the practice was fraught with hidden dangers: 'The brush is an instrument which, if used wrongly, can seriously damage the hair, but if correctly used can beautify and contribute to the health of the hair.'[1] The most important advice beauty writers had to offer, however, was to keep all of this women's work hidden from masculine eyes. Feminine beauty might take up a lot of time and effort but any administrations to the self had to be invisible, otherwise the spell would be broken, so 'Whether you shampoo your hair at home, or have it done outside, is a matter for you to decide. Shampoo your hair when you husband is not at home. Most men are interested in results, not in how you obtain them. Do not discuss your methods with your husband. He will be aware that you do have a permanent and hair settings, but he wants only to admire the finished effect. Will you remember this? Because when you have learned it well an apply it always, you will know the most vital secret of feminine seductiveness.'[2]

[1] Foan, p.88

[2] Dengel, p.29

These notions of feminine beauty, however, were white and to be considered really beautiful black women had to conform to these ideals as much as possible, in particular by straightening their hair or getting a 'process'. Hair had to be tidy and straightened hair was the mark of a 'respectable' black women; it was an important part of the etiquette of good grooming. Justine Henderson remembered that in the 1950s, 'You always knew that it was not a good thing to have nappy hair. You always straightened it. One of the first things you learned about taking care of your own hair was how to straighten it. Nobody ever said why you couldn't go outside with your hair washed, but you learned very early on that you couldn't. I always knew once you washed your hair, until it

[1] Maxine Craig, 'The decline and fall of the conk; or how to read a process', FASHION THEORY, Vol. 1 Issue 4, December 1997, p.41

[2] Dengel, p.35

was straightened, you put a scarf on it.'[1]

The notion of a smooth head of hair being the beauty ideal was so pervasive that even white hair which superficially resembled black was described in racist terms, particularly in the 1950s, when an unruffled finish was the look to aim for. Women were supposed to brush their hair regularly, to 'work for smoothness, even when the hair is worn loose. There is nothing attractive about Borneo bushiness.'[2]

This white civilizing process was applied to the hair of the first wave of immigrants to Britain in the 1950s, and as a similar attitude had existed in America a lot of specialist hair products were imported, such as the Yvette Home Hair Straightening Kit and the later European products Teda and Magic Hair Straight, although many black women resorted to a hot comb and grease to achieve the desired effect. The popular hair relaxants, like their skin lightening counter-parts, can be summed up as devices for making the hair look as white as possible, an attitude which could also be seen expressed in American fashion and beauty magazines targeting a black female audience. For instance, a 1959 guide to grooming for 'Negro girls' published in America advised, 'You are exactly like any other girl, but you think there is a difference and the difference shows. When we come to the discussion of hair, you feel pretty sure that this is where the difference begins ... and you're anxious to do something about it. Sure, it has made you wonder many times ... why did I have to have this kind of hair? You're not alone with such thoughts ... many girls have hair that is so tightly curled that they too must resort to hair straightening methods ... the burden may be easier when you know you don't carry it alone. Instead of wishing for the "fairy godmother" to come down and touch you with her magic wand that will give you a new kind of hair ... work for a head of hair you'll be proud of.' The orthodoxy of the late 1950s was that black women should always straighten their hair or, if unsuccessful in this practice, wear a wig. Straightening was an arduous business and lasted only until the hair was dampened, so living with typical British weather meant the whole idea of regular straightening was fairly relentless. This was a problem confined not just to Britain. A woman living in New York remembered, 'The bane of all little black girls is the water. I went with my grandmother to a church picnic and I loved to swim. And I remember coming back in a bus with the other kids and hearing people whispering in the back about my hair looking like Brillo Pads. I remember feeling really hurt, but not particularly knowing what to do.'[1] Not all women in America followed these rigorously imposed beauty standards, though, and Robin D. G. Kelly[2] has found examples in the late 1950s of hair worn *au naturel* by some avant-garde middle-class women of the black bohemia. There are isolated examples of this in Britain, particularly amongst the Soho-Boho crowd involved in the modern jazz scene, but on the whole white standards predominated.

White women involved in the same avant-garde arenas wore short urchin cuts, but this bohemian Left Bank look was fairly short-lived. By the late 1950s big hair was *de rigueur*. The long, rather full hair-styles had become increasingly stylized into the beehive, a bouffanted cone shape or high puffball that rose from the head. The height of the hair was achieved with the use of big rollers, backcombing or 'teasing' it furiously, a process originally used in the 1930s on a less exaggerated scale and called French combing. Each lock of hair was

[1] Craig, 'The decline and fall of the conk, p.401

[2] Robin D. G. Kelly, 'Nap Time: Historicizing the afro', FASHION THEORY, Vol. 1, Issue 4, December 1997, p.341

combed back on itself until the hair stood vertically, then carefully patted into place and fixed with lashings of lacquer without losing any of its height. Occasionally hair was built up around plastic or wire frames for added effect. The remaining hair was set on rollers to create the 'flip', the curling of the hair outwards just below the ears and, for the very flamboyant, a curl or guiche was set in place on both cheeks. The structure could also be given texture with a perm or extra hairpieces called switches. To keep the bouffant viable as long as possible, hairnets were worn by day and curlers at night, although the practice was frowned upon and more appropriately feminine alternatives were suggested, such as, 'tie your head in a piece of coloured tulle, or a wide silk ribbon tied on top with a perky bow. Don't use those horrible brown nets for night wear if you want to be attractive.'[1]

[1] Dengel, p.35

Patricia Sartory with an urchin cut, mid-1950s

Michael Cox with a 'jazz-inspired' haircut, mid-1950s

There were several variations of the bouffant hair-style but they had the same thing in common: a high puffed-up effect held in place by the new aerosol hairsprays which came out of the needs for insecticide during the Pacific War. Antoine had been one of the first to use hair lacquer on a professional basis, a technique copied from a group of Chinese actors who had performed in Paris in the 1920s. He observed how hair fixative was used to give their dramatic hair-styles a sculptured appearance and appropriated this heavy treatment, which literally glued the hair in place, to keep formal, evening hair-dos intact. The problem was that it was sticky and difficult to remove; only white spirit could budge it, which didn't help the condition of the client's hair. It wasn't until the early 1950s that hairsprays began to improve when shellac was dissolved in alcohol and put into aerosols. As the can was sprayed, the alcohol dissolved, leaving a thin film of shellac to hold the hair, which stayed stuck fast until the next shampoo and made the most extravagant of bouffant styles possible. By 1963 plastic-based hairsprays had taken over from shellac, the most popular brands manufactured by Goya, Gala and Henry C. Miner.

On looking back at these seemingly eccentric styles of the 1950s, some writers read into them a subservient, domesticated femininity. McCracken, for instance, sees the bouffant as a representation of the traditional status and conventionality of women in the late 1950s: 'the perfect symbol of women and nature. Uncontrolled, women's hair was everything women were: organic, expressive, emotional, spontaneous, transformational and sensual. Controlled, it was everything women (and nature) were supposed to become: meek, unthreatening, compliant and disciplined.

Variations of the 'Bingle' by Xavier, c. 1960s

The Pagoda Line by Austin Gerard, 1963

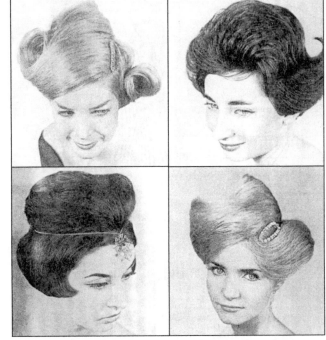

The Pagoda Line

[1] McCracken, p.36

Hair was the perfect playing field for the 1950s version of the war between the sexes.'[1] Although bouffants can be regarded as symbols of servitude, imprisoning the 'naturalness' of women, this in itself is a rather essentialist proposition. McCracken seems to be particularly perturbed by the thought of women damaging their hair to achieve an artificialized effect, complaining that hair in the 1950s ended up looking like a synthetic material rather than its natural state. These bouffanted styles could be reinterpreted, on the other hand, as the apex of 1950s and early 1960s technological optimism, when the synthetic was praised over the natural and the Western world believed wholeheartedly in the progress

185

made possible by science, an attitude normally associated with the geometric styles of Vidal Sassoon and his followers. The bouffant styles were using the best advances in technology hairdressing had to offer and were looking to a Utopian future rather than an austere war-ridden past, literally pointing to the sky, where new jetplanes sped past and rockets zoomed. And why should carefully constructed, artificial styles be regarded as automatically subservient?

Punk women, for instance, could be seen as some of the most assertive in terms of their sartorial statements and certainly did not seem to be bothered by damaging their hair to acquire the achieved effect. One of the most iconic bouffant wearers in the late 1950s and early 1960s was Brigitte Bardot, who was a symbol of sexual freedom, albeit a rather conservative example, and was a powerful role model for many women of all classes across Europe. The style was definitely not one of servitude.

By the early 1960s increasing numbers of women began to dress their hair at home rather than attending a professional hairdresser's for a shampoo and set, using hair rollers to create their own curls and waves. Hairdressers realized they had to find ways to fight back and increase custom. To persuade the resistant consumer that salons were the places to be if one wanted to be in fashion, geometrically styled haircuts were pushed in a bid to replace the backcombed beehive with swinging, shining hair. Sophisticated perming and cutting techniques, which required an expert hairdresser such as Sassoon and Leonard and regular visits to the salon for their successful upkeep, were also promoted in the pages of popular women's fashion magazines and the trade press to get women back into contact with the hairdresser. Extravagant shapes like the Pagoda Line of 1963 show the lengths some stylists were prepared to go to woo women who had no hope of copying such looks at home. The battle of the geometric cut versus the soufflé, a softer variation on the permed and set look, also preoccupied hairdressing trade magazines such as *Hair and Beauty* throughout the mid- to late 1960s. In July 1966 a competition was held by the

Silvio Camillo: 'If God had intended a geometric look he would have made women with square faces, square breasts, square legs and square eyes . . . Curve is coming back into hairdressing again: it is curve and movement, not curls and waves.'

Geometric v. Soufflé

Fellowship of Hair Artists in which members were invited to show examples of the geometric or soufflé styles and then defend their respective positions. The hairdresser Xavier, firmly in the soufflé camp, flatly argued that the whole argument was out of date, the soufflé had won: 'Fashion editors have not given the geometric any publicity for the last six months. They are searching desperately for a new image.' Silvio Camillo, anther stylist committed to the soufflé, commented, 'If God had intended a geometric look he would have made women with square faces, square breasts, square legs and square eyes ... Curve is coming back into hairdressing again.' But Gerard London counterattacked, 'Why ruffle it all up when we have reached a perfection with scissors and comb?'[1]

[1] HAIR AND BEAUTY, July 1966, p.9

For the British male the short back and sides was still the norm, although 'continental' styling, characterized by short razor-tapered hair, was fashionable amongst many young men. Elaborate hair-dos for women were no longer status symbols but indicative of working-class trash and by the late 1960s between sixteen and twenty-four women, in particular were identified as a target group who were becoming increasingly resistant to regular professional hairdressing. They styled their hair themselves at home, although hairdressers such as Leonard were marginally successful in introducing new styles for teenagers with the gamine look, as modelled by Twiggy (Lesley Hornby) in 1966. This seminal British haircut, photographed by Barry Lategan, was the result of an eight-hour session in 1966 at the hands of Leonard (who had once sold second-hand cars in Putney) and the colourist Daniel Galvin. Justin de Villeneuve, her manager and partner at the time, described the event: 'Lesley was

Twiggy.
Hair by Leonard.
Photographed by
Barry Lategan, 1966.

Twiggy

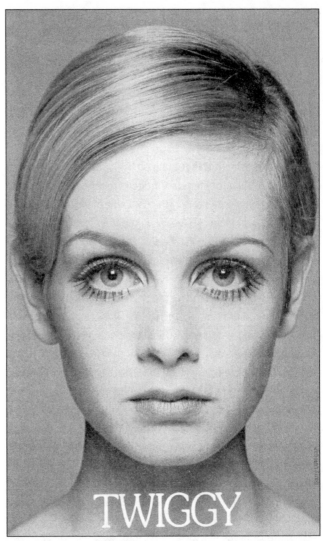

there the whole day. Hair cut short, not finished so Daniel could put in highlights, then downstairs for Uncle Len to finish it off. When he'd finished a pin could have dropped and you would have heard it out in the street. Clients, models, staff cleaners, tea boys, receptionists were all speechless. It was like a magic moment in a corny movie. Leonard had created a minor miracle. Up to then Lesley's barnet had been stringy and in poor condition, what with her trying different products ... Leonard had sculpted a little golden cap. The child looked a cross between an angel and Greta Garbo.'[1]

[1] De Villeneuve, p.44

It was at this time that inexpensive synthetic wigs began to catch on. Developments in modern technology had made convincing synthetic acrylic fibre or Dynel hair available and cheap and funky fun styles by companies such as Fashion Tress began to be worn openly as fashion rather than disguise. Most cheap wigs were manufactured in Hong Kong, although the more expensive real hair was still being imported from mainland China. Hairdressers realized that there was a potential for increasing the business with the selling of artificial hair and optimistically asserted: ' Wigs and hairpieces have captured feminine fancy completely and irresistibly. No grooming trend in recent years has come even close in popularity and acceptance. Hairdressers are uniquely qualified to sell and service hair goods. They should be used to give complete satisfaction to patrons and considerable profit to themselves. Every shop has some feminine employees. They can wear wigs or different arrangements of hairpieces. No shop is busy, every hour, every day. There are many times when operators have nothing to do but talk or loll about. Such unproductive time can be turned to advantage. Use it to service wigs and hairpieces.'[2] By 1968 there was a wig boom. Factories were at full stretch exporting millions of pounds' worth of wigs to

Fantasy wig, 1960s

[2] Cordwell, p.92

Wiglets, 1960s

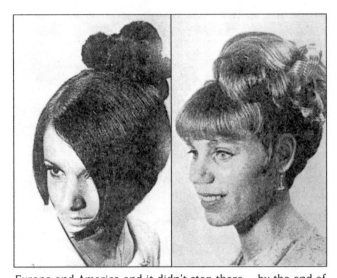

Europe and America and it didn't stop there — by the end of the 1960s one third of all European women owned a 'wig of convenience'[1] and these were definitely not cover-ups for thinning hair. *Hair and Beauty* magazine applauded the far-sighted nature of the Birmingham Co-op, which in 1966 added a wig section to their main salon in one store, selling fashion wigs at prices ranging from wiglets at six guineas to machine-made transformations with handmade fronts from twenty-three pounds, and by 1969 it was acknowledged that the colour of one's hair was no longer a natural given when HM Customs and Immigration deemed it unnecessary to declare the colour of hair on British passports. Arlene Dahl's guide to femininity, ALWAYS ASK A MAN, advised wig wearers to put their natural hair in pin curls close to the head when wearing a wig, otherwise 'with the added bulk underneath you might resemble a balloon'.[2]

Men tended to wear wigs differently, moving further and

[1] Lois Gurel and Marianne Beeson, eds, DIMENSIONS OF DRESS AND ADORNMENT: A BOOK OF READINGS (Toronto, third edition Kendall/Hunt Publishers, 1979)

[2] Arlene Dahl, ALWAYS ASK A MAN: ARLENE DAHL'S KEY TO FEMININITY (London, Frederick Miller Ltd, 1965), p.93

Serventi salons, 1963

further towards the naturalism women were rejecting,
although there was an attempt to introduce a bit of fun into
their appearance. Lisa Wigs, a wig boutique in America, had
enormous success in 1968 when they marketed a fake
moustache and beard set for two hundred dollars to

transform the executive man into an instant swinger – if he was really lucky he might even find a Tarzan chest wig. Barbershops in London also tried to get a bit more 'with it'. Samson and Delilah, an establishment off Bond Street run by Denise Karen, had two female cutters attending to their male customers in black bikini tops and matching loincloths and at Leonard Ludwin's of May's Court a man could buy artificial sideburns. By the late 1960s men were prepared to enter the female domain of the open salon, which was marketed under the term 'unisex hairdressing'. This not only gestured towards the supposed breaking down of sexual conventions but could provide the forum for an erotic encounter. One male writer panted, 'Many women's salons are providing a his 'n' hers service. Men and women sit side by side at the washbasins or under the dryer and nobody seems unduly conscious or bothered by the presence of the opposite sex. You are just as likely to have an attractive blonde or appealing brunette easing comb and scissors through your hair. You may even date her afterwards.'[1] Sassoon opened a male salon in Knightsbridge in 1968 but the most infamous new haunt for the modern man was Sweeny's of Beauchamp Place and its sister salon, Todd's of King's Road, Chelsea, named after the demon barber of Fleet Street and run by Gary Craze. This groovy, happening salon was 'in a basement furnished with antiques, noisy and often full of well-known personalities: actors, dress designers, pop singers, various peers and a duke. You can buy groovy Herbert Johnson hats and even eat there. Todd's is in a row of Georgian-type houses, presently being renovated, near World's End. Gary lives there as well, and when pop or Eastern music – the air is heavy with incense – doesn't satisfy you, it is possible you

[1] Rodney Bennett-England, AS YOUNG AS YOU LOOK: MALE GROOMING AND REJUVENATION (London, Peter Owen Limited), 1970, p.106

195

When you've seen ⟨salon⟩
you've seen them all!
Britain's finest range of dryers
⟨salon⟩
Ask your wholesaler or write for details to
Salon (Nelson) Limited, Holin Bank, Brierfield, Lancashire

**Advertisement for
Salon hair-dryers,
c. 1960s**

may find Mick Jagger or another star sitting in the next chair.'[1]
The skills of the barber were changing. He used to be a
technician in charge of his Bressant clippers; now he had to
be a male stylist, a rejuvenator of fashionable masculinity in
the swinging cities of the 1960s, where hair salons for men
were mushrooming, with appropriately trendy names like
Mane Line, Scissors and Beau Brummell. Rodney Bennett-
England commented on this change in 1970:

'The old barber's shops resembled sheep-shearing shacks in
the Australian bush, with hair clippings all over the floor. In
them haircutting was a dull routine, if sometimes chancy,
operation. You were in and out in under fifteen minutes, the
wiser for a smutty joke or two, lighter of a few shillings, and
relieved that the dreary session would not have to be
repeated for a couple of weeks or so. The décor was often
decidedly shabby, with uncomfortable chairs to wait on, drab
linoleum floors, and display cases full of faded hair creams

[1] Ibid.

and contraceptive products. Today's salon presents a very different picture. A man's attitude towards his hair is almost summed up by whether he still talks of his barber or his hairdresser. Many salons now resemble gentlemen's clubs with deep, comfortable armchairs, wood-panelled walls and pictures or prints. Others are close-carpeted, with chandeliers, potted plants and piped music. In some you can order gin and tonic or coffee and soft drinks; in others you can easily while away a complete half-day having your hair heightened, lightened and brightened, your hands manicured and your tired face cleansed and patted back into new vigour.'[1] Prince Philip and Field Marshal Viscount Montgomery may still have been going to Truefitt and Hill of Old Bond Street but Leonard had Tony Blackburn!

[1] Bennett-England, p.104

Despite all this frantic repositioning, the relationship between the hairdresser and the client was beginning to completely break down. Women were increasingly liberated from the confines of the salon, choosing to style their own hair in the comfort of their own home, helped by the introduction of inexpensive hand-held hair-dryers and stand dryers for domestic use. The permed and set look began to be regarded as a style for middle-aged mothers. All a modern woman needed was a good cut and a quick blow-dry in the bedroom, instead of recoursing to what became known as the 'sausage machine salon' where the client collected a gown, walked to the shampoo basin, then to the setting table and then to the drying bay. After yet another walk to the combing-out unit, women preferred the sanctity of their homes to the impersonality of the salon as factory. To further exacerbate the problem, the British press began a concerted campaign against the hairdressing profession in 1966, commenting rather unflatteringly on inefficiency, unhygienic practices and overcharging. The women's magazine *Annabel* published an article headlined 'Is hairdressing a racket?' and the *Sunday Times* colour supplement singled out four British professions in which a 'get-rich-quick, easy-money mentality prevailed:' barrow boys, burglars, prostitutes and hairdressers! By the time *Reveille* wrote of the 'dirty, undisciplined, take-it-or-leave-it atmosphere of the majority of average priced salons', the Hairdressers' Publicity Group had been set up to launch a counter-offensive against the 'ugly smears on the reputation of an honest and hardworking profession'.[1] Even so, the image of the profession had never sunk so low. The potential client had to be persuaded to come back to the salon by being convinced it was part of a happening scene rather than a rather boring place to have a trim. Salons could be art galleries, places to have astrological readings, hair personality analysis, tannings, facials, even indoor putting greens. To counteract the grim appearance of the 1960s open-plan salon, hooded dryers with built-in music were introduced which could be operated by the client, and Scandinavian wood effects were used in the décor. One modern salon had some of the female dryers 'frilled and be-ribboned in stiffened lace hats whilst others were bedecked in broderie anglais lace caps', but even this 'delicious bit of frippery' failed to deter the march of the alternative countercultural styles which were much easier to tend at home. By 1966 *Hair and Beauty* stated that the 'demand for perming of any type, appears to have reached an absoloute nadir'. Men and women, both black and white, were allowing their hair to grow long and 'natural', exaggerating pop styles like the Beatles' moptop, originally created by Astrid

[1] HAIR AND BEAUTY, January 1967, p.32

A 'happening' salon, c.1960s

Kirchnerr in the early 1960s when the group was playing in Hamburg. The hippie style imported from California became popular in the late 1960s, a look described by the writer David Horowitz: 'People looked different. Peace symbols and crystal pendants had replaced crucifixes and Stars of David as emblems of religious conviction. Clothes were tie-dyed and bucolic, colours psychedelic, and hair long. Women were going bra-less ... and a band, booming through amplified speakers produced an effect something like entering a new dimension. I felt: a new world is possible.'

The wheel had turned full circle, long hair, a boon to hairdressers before the 1920s, was now regarded as the beginning of the end for the trade. The hairdresser George Michael commented, 'As women develop more expertise in caring for their own hair, as weekly standing appointments become rarer and rarer, most salons can only make real money by giving haircuts — certainly not by letting hair grow. Short hair has to be cut, "styled" every six weeks or so to keep it looking well, whereas long hair only has to be trimmed slightly almost every two months. And this is a trimming, it cannot be called a styling, which is more expensive.'[1] Hair was no longer a form of conspicuous consumption, a shoring up of the advantages of capitalism, but an important means of expressing dissatisfaction with establishment culture and showing there was an alternative if old restrictions could be overturned. A hair androgyny began to sweep the Western world; there were no rules over who could have long hair now because, as Germaine Greer put it, 'Everybody had hair and lots of it, floating round their heads like smoke.'[2] Long hair was a revolution, like freedom of speech, worn by demonstrators against Vietnam, promotors of drug culture

[1] George Michael & Rue Lindsay, GEORGE MICHAEL'S SECRETS FOR BEAUTIFUL HAIR, (New York, Doubleday and Co, 1981), p.159

[2] '1968 and all that', INDEPENDENT ON SUNDAY, 8 February 1998, p.12

and fetishized in lyrics such as these from the popular hippie musical *Hair*:

Hair, hair, hair, hair, hair, hair, hair, hair,
Flow it, show it, long as God can grow it, my hair,
I want it long, straight, curly, fuzzy, snaggy, shaggy,
Ratty, matty, oily, greasy, fleecy, shining, gleaming,
   steaming,
Flaxen, waxen, knotted, polka-dotted,
Twisted, beaded, braided, powdered, flowered and
   confettied,
Bangled, tangled, spangled and spaghettied.

Long hair was rebellious, the white middle-class visual equivalent of the black afro; short hair was reactionary. The crew cut, dubbed by Sassoon 'the disease of the scalp', was an extreme American look which seemed to express all that was wrong about the repressed masculinity of the post-war male psyche which had exhibited itself in a rabid military imperialism. Long-haired men were viewed with the utmost suspicion by the Great British public primarily because the strict boundaries of gendered hair which had existed for most of the twentieth century were being breached and this was threatening. The man with long hair was suggesting that he had thought about it, had made a conscious decision not to have an Ordinary or Continental, and the presumption of male vanity was a difficult concept to accept in a reticent British culture. Real men were not overly concerned about the fashionability of their appearance, so long-haired men had to be anarchists, effeminate or perhaps both. There were also the connotations of dirtiness to contend with. Short hair

George Michael, a hairdresser who specialized in long hair from the 1960s to the 1980s

had been the preserve of the stinking poor who cluttered up the workhouse in the nineteenth century; now it was the turn of the long-haired man. This was reinforced by the hippie's self-conscious identification with poverty in the form of wrinkled bell bottoms and unkempt beards, all causing the usual furore. Like the bob, long hair on men was visual evidence of gender in transition; men and women were beginning to look the same. The editor of the trade publication *Tailor and Cutter* had stern words about this worrying trend, believing that 'adopting girl's hair-styles may lead to adopting their clothes and there is a danger in that'.[1] Despite the attacks, the long-haired look had become the orthodoxy by the end of the 1960s, when even middle-aged straights were prepared to have a lick of hair curling onto their jacket collars. Greer, like many women, also found it irritating that men could have better hair than them, describing 'many young men sport[ing] full heads of tossing curls and long, glossy tresses which their sisters try vainly to emulate. The old supposition that women grow thicker and longer hair on their heads than men cannot die painlessly. The long-haired men are called freaks and perverts, and women resort to immense cascades of store-bought hair to redress the balance.'[2] The influence of hippie hair, with its espousal of simple natural styles, severely threatened the already beleaguered hairdresser, despite attempts to incorporate countercultural ideas about hair into their craft through the commercialization of herbal shampoos such as Culpeper's and old-fashioned therapies such as head massage, which smacked of the nostalgic hippie aesthetic. The emphasis began to be on hair health and some hairdressers openly sold themselves as benign dictators who wouldn't cut hair but would nurture it instead. George Michael, for example, espoused a pseudo-hippie aesthetic of deep spiritual empathy with hair: 'No matter how well thought out her decision is, no matter how sensible the change seems to be, when she sits down in the chair for "The Rape of the Lock", it's a very traumatic time. That hair has

[1] TAILOR AND CUTTER, 27 January 1967, p.98

[2] Germaine Greer, THE FEMALE EUNUCH, (London, Paladin, 1971) p.27

been touching the woman's body, her breasts, her back: it has given sexual pleasure and sensual feelings not only to her but her man. It is almost like one of her children. I have to cut that hair with love, not anger, and I have to treat the hair very carefully. I have to handle that hair as if it is still a beautiful ornament, and I have to love it while I cut it.'[1] Not all women were as liberated as they would have wished, though, as the long heads of hair had to be shiny and smooth, as in Sassoon's high-contrast photographs, which promoted a glossy finish styled to emphasize movement. To achieve this look many women went to their local salon to have their hair wrapped, a process whereby the hair was literally wrapped flat against the head and pinned until dry to achieve a poker-straight effect, or ironed their hair at home.

This promotion of a 'natural' look was mirrored in black hair-styles. By the 1960s black hair was normally straightened, greased, backcombed and sprayed, so that it did anything but look curly, and American magazines such as *Ebony* contained advertisements for hair straighteners, instant hair or wigs, thereby strengthening this orthodoxy. This process had become such a matter of course that to see a black woman with nappy hair was regarded as peculiar, a feeling expanded upon in an article *Ebony* carried in June 1966 called 'The Natural Look: New Modes for Negro Women': 'A Frenchman who had been in this country but a short time was astonished to encounter on the street one day a shapely, brown-skinned woman whose close-cropped, rough-textured hair was in marked contrast to that of Brigitte Bardot – or any other woman he'd ever seen. Intrigued by her extraordinarily curly locks, he rushed up to her and blurted in Gallic impulsiveness: "But I thought only Negro men had curly hair ... " An increasing

Joan Armatrading with an 'authentic' 1970s Afro

number of Negro women are turning their backs on traditional concepts of style and beauty by wearing their hair in its naturally kinky state. Though they remain a relatively small group, confined primarily to the trend-making cities of New York and Chicago, they are frequently outspoken, and always aware of definite reasons why they decided to "go natural".[1]

[1] Arthur Marwick, BEAUTY IN HISTORY, (London, Thames and Hudson, 1988), p.365

White women too had to beware of any curls escaping from their set heads — kinky hair was a real problem — but beauty writers were there, as always, to give advice: 'To overcome kinky or curly hair, saturate it with a medium to heavy wave lotion or a non-accelerated cream straightener, and set the hair in large curls, stretching it over the rollers as you work. While most women will have to rely on bigger and smoother rollers and smoother, straighter permanents to rule their waves, others will be helped by new chemical hair straighteners and an · *un*-curling iron with built-in conditioner. But these are best handled by a professional, two or three times a year.'[1] The products used to create this 'correct' look were dangerous to say the least. June Watson of CJ's salon, a stylist of Afro-Caribbean hair since the 1960s, described the process: 'We had to check for strength, porosity and abrasions on the scalp, because the relaxing agent was sodium hydroxide, which burns. We'd have to grease or base the scalp so it wouldn't burn.'[2] Increasingly, though, the straightened look was regarded as endemic of the racism which was seen to pervade American society in the late 1960s and a more authentic look began to be espoused. Straightened hair was a sign of false consciousness amongst American blacks and the beauty of a 'natural' blackness was exhorted through the Black is Beautiful movement, a rejection of the enslavement of many Americans to white beauty ideals. Authentically black hair-styles such as the Afro, called the Natural in America, were seen as more correct, an espousal of a rather essentialist look which bears comparison with radical feminism's stance on fashion and provided a crossover look in the style of Angela Davis.

The influence of the Black is Beautiful movement in the

[1] Dahl, p.85

[2] THE INDEPENDENT ON SUNDAY, 1996

USA led to white culture beginning to question the notion that whiteness was the epitome of beauty, and obversely indicators of blackness were appropriated by the white avant-garde in the guise of the radical chic look and eventually trickled down to mainstream fashion. Black looks influenced white hair-styles to such an extent that curly perms became popular and one could buy the Supreme Afro or Freedom wig from the back pages of the *New Musical Express* in 1975. Some British men found the look difficult — Justin de Villeneuve, the manager and partner of the model Twiggy throughout most of the 'Swinging Sixties', described an off-putting encounter with the radically hirsute Yoko Ono: 'The first time I met Yoko in the flesh, so to speak, was at the *Yellow Submarine* premiere. When we got into the back of the limo I thought I was being attacked by a giant Brillo Pad. It was Yoko's Afro pubic hair-style, a fuzzy-wuzzy gone crackers! Twiggs and I couldn't breathe with the old barnet up our nasers.'[1] Some hairdressers were very averse to this voodoo-child look, 'A current fad is permanenting to give the effect of the frizzies or an Afro. Well I'm not in favour of frizzies. If you achieve this frizz via artificial means it could represent almost total destruction of the hair.'[2]

[1] De Villeneuve, p.94

[2] Michael, pp.106–7

By the early 1970s the imagery and language of counterculture had been co-opted to sell hair products which espoused 'freedom' and 'liberty' for women who no longer had to resort to backcombing and hair spray. Sales of perms, one of the main income generators of the hairdressing profession, had plummeted as a result of the general fashion for smoothness and were further dented with the invention of Carmen heated rollers. On 1 January 1971, in an optimistic start to the new year, the *Hairdressers' Weekly Journal* had on its cover the plaintive legend 'Your opportunity to bring back the perm', but it was not to be, because by now the majority of men and women had gradually let their hair down whether hippies or not. A few were optimistic about this change, seeing it as especially liberating for the stiff-upper-lipped British male, who could now be less reticent about embracing new fashions in hair, one writing, 'Hair-styles now have more variety and allow the male to choose a style which best suits and expresses his personality. Fashions in hair vary, of course, from age to age. Men generally are wearing their hair longer — perhaps as a reaction against the short-back-and-sides, a hangover from the last war. Long hair generally flatters the male, gives him a younger look and is aesthetically more pleasing.'[1]

[1] Bennett-England, p.103

This was to be the beginning of a whole new era.

(4)

MILL

ENN-
TOWARDS THE
IUM

Pop music and dance culture had their effects on British hair in the 1970s. To offset the Torremollinos tan lit up by the glitterball on the disco floor, highlighting caught on. Just like blondeness, streaked hair has undergone different levels of meanings and was regarded as something to be avoided right up to the 1950s, when it was given the rather ladylike name of frosting. In the early years of the twentieth century sun-streaked hair, like the tan, was seen as indicative of manual

**David and Angie
Bowie, 1972**

workers, those who had to labour outside for a living rather then residing inside and cultivating a leisured paleness. Even though Coco Chanel had publicized a sun-kissed look, this was still confined to fashionable circles in the early 1930s, when Gilbert Foan advised against exposing the hair to the elements and dubbed the malaise 'holiday scalp'. He warned that 'during the holiday season many of our clients manifest serious symptoms arising from sun-dried hair and excessively parched scalps. In some instances the disorder takes the form

of sun-bleached hair-strands, portions of the longer hair
being blanched to a yellow or strawish hue.'[1] By the 1970s
attempting to induce holiday scalp was all the rage and
bottles of Sun In destroyed many a head of hair on a cheap
charter holiday in the Greek islands. Together with a deep
orange tan and a halter-neck top to show it off, this was the
look in which to strut your stuff. Hairdressers were warned to
go steadily to avoid their clients looking like rejects from
Studio 54, for 'when streaking or frosting isn't done properly,
the effect is garish, overstated, rather like an elegant car
gone wrong with too many flamboyant accessories, rally
stripes, and the like. If you're going to streak or frost, make
sure it's done correctly, or don't do it at all.'[2]

Men were at last prepared to enter the debate over
whether to dye their hair and the new ideas spread to an
older generation. Clairol had made great strides in America in
the late 1960s, persuading men to use colour when it showed
signs of grey with slogans like 'help make an old man young
again' for the product Great Day. The psychological effects of
this treatment were emphasized rather than the notion of
beautification and businessmen testified to the success they
had in the workplace after disguising their grey hairs, getting
big orders and new clients as a result of their more youthful
looks. Hair tinting was the way forward. Manufacturers in
Britain responded with Grecian 2000, essentially a dye for
grey hair although this was never explicit in its advertising.
The title of the product conflated the glories of the civilized
golden age of Ancient Greek Classicism with a progressive
Utopian future, to appeal to a sophisticated masculinity
rather than feminine narcissism.

[1] Foan, p.437

[2] Michael, p.93

211

Glam rockers like Roy Wood, who provided a hilarious segue between hippie and androgyny with his multi-coloured and backcombed locks, and David Bowie had no fear of hair dye, incorporating it into two of the most memorable hairstyles of the decade. In 1972 Bowie's hair was a luminous orange, cut short and spiky on the top and kept long at the back, although this mutated into the reviled Mullet by the 1980s and was worn by musclebound beery types and faded footballers. Rather than a fish, the Mullet was a term given to a man's bi-level hair-style that was short in the front and long

Mullet, 1980s

**Permed mullet, 1980s
Photography by
Richard Lohr**

at the back, the name invented by Michael Diamond, a member of the American rap group the Beastie Boys and presented in an issue of their fanzine, *Grand Royal*. The article had spawned a veritable Mullet industry on the Internet by the late 1990s with myriad websites from Eye on the Mullet, The North American Mullet Page to the Mullet Research Expedition of 1997, which asked for reports of Mullet sightings and gave advice on what to ask for to achieve the right effect at the barbers – 'One on the sides, don't touch the back, six on the top and don't cut it wack, Jack.' Teen America seemed

213

fascinated by the tension engendered by a haircut that was in both camps, short on top for crew-cut neatness and the back long, for a nod in the direction of hippie counterculture, and gave the cut a host of alternative names displaying its ethnic origins and the perceived mentality or uncoolness of its adoptees, such as Ape Drape, Guido, Soccer Rocker and Hack Job. The Mullet was essentially a survivor, adapting to fashion in the late 1970s when a long strand of plaited hair was grown at the back, dyed for added effect, and appeared in various cyber guises in the 1980s, such as the Mohican plus Mullet in the band Sigue Sigue Sputnik. In the 1990s it seemed to have finally settled on the heads of fashion-impaired celebrities such as the nightclub king Peter Stringfellow and American soft rock stars such as Michael Bolton, who used it to disguise thinning locks.

Trevor Sorbie was responsible for one of the other innovative and copied haircuts of the decade. In 1974, whilst working as creative director at Sassoon's, Sorbie created the wedge, a hair uniform adopted by 'southern English, club-going, working-class soul stylists'[1] to go with Fiorucci peg-top trousers, white socks and low-cut loafers before punk reared its anarchic head. With a side parting and a floppy fringe which swept round to the back, this was a masterpiece of cutting, dyed darker underneath to emphasize its wedginess. Peter York described how to achieve the look: 'When they first cut it and blow it dry they keep on brushing the sides flat, pushing them back underneath the long bits at the crown, so the bob part of it is resting on the pushed-back horizontal part. The stylist's trick then is to let it go, so it springs out, the long bits bouncing out on top of the side, all that bouncing volume disappearing into razored flatness with

[1] Peter York, MODERN TIMES, p.72, (London, Futura, 1985)

**Sigue Sigue Sputnik,
forerunners of
Cyberpunk, 1980s
Photography by
Derek Ridgers**

215

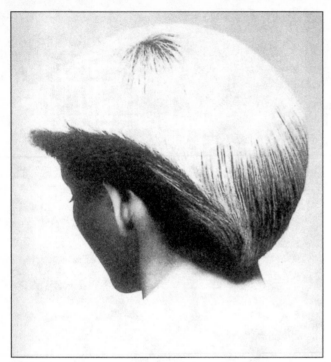

**Wedge haircut by
Trevor Sorbie for
Vidal Sassoon, 1974**

nothing hippie or impromptu around the neck. Bare necks, visible ears, with bouncing subversive hair top. What could be more irritating than this long-short combination?"[1]

    In the late 1970s a new interpretation of the blonde look came with the emergence of punk. Alternative images were sourced for their shock value and a band called the Moors Murderers played on the discredited bottle-blonde style of Myra Hindley. Here, obvious chemically enhanced blondeness was clearly associated with criminality. First Ruth Ellis, then Hindley, in one of the most famous media representations of blondeness in Britain, were responsible for reinstating all that was cheap, nasty and, in the public's

[1] York, p.72

imagination, ultimately evil about the look. Hindley's cheap, blonde bouffant signified her unnaturalness, the woman with no maternal instinct, the child killer. Accordingly, in their public project of *épater la bourgeois* punk women embodied all that was artificial over natural and seized on the deliberately cheap and tacky – their heavily painted faces bore witness to this, but the use of bleach took the look one step further. Following on from Debbie Harry's experimentation with blonde hair with obviously dark roots – something in earlier days which would have signified slovenliness, the same as going out to the corner shop in slippers and hair curlers under a see-through net scarf – this had now become the height of alternative chic. Punk girls wore white pancake make-up, refusing to embody the glowing good health of the models in fashion magazines, and paraded black roots on obviously peroxided hair with pride. This trash aesthetic was built on by British punks and transmuted into various types: the white blonde bouffant as worn by Jordan, the shop assistant at Sex, the yellow blonde Mohican and the bleaching of the hair as a prelude to using Crazy Colour. Punk attacked the prevailing natural look in the mid-1970s, rejecting the sanitized blonde streaks held in place by Brut hair spray and the aspirational glamour of Farrah Fawcett Majors, whose haircut starred in the USA import *Charlie's Angels*. This rather orthodox version of feminine hair-styling, the Californian blonde flick, was rejected by punk women, who were deliberately artificial, disavowing society's judgements on what was deemed a correctly feminine appearance and supplanting it with a look associated with pornographic, particularly fetishistic, representation. An area traditionally signifying womens'

Debbie Harry, late 1970s

subordination was reappropriated as subversion; bleached blonde hair with obviously dark roots now signalled female rebellion. Conventional prettiness was ignored in favour of a threatening, tribal look. Traditional ideas of beauty and taste in women's appearance were deliberately avoided and styling was anti-natural, despite, or precisely because of, the natural look that was prevalent in high fashion at that time, in the guise of the tweed hacking jacket and mainstream peasant look. Punk was not in good taste or wholesome but seized upon the cheap and tacky. To choose so explicitly not to look natural was an aggressive gesture and its power was so potent it was appropriated within late 1970s dress, so that by the early 1980s neon streaks in punk-styled hair were more likely to be the badge of a student anarchist or middle-aged radical feminist.[1]

**The Californian blonde
by Clairol**

Experimental punk hair-styles which relied on the impact of verticality led to the use of sugar, flour or soap and water to give the desired spiky effect. As the looks became incorporated into hairdressing culture by the late 1970s, manufacturers responded with a whole new range of fixative products which were more consumer-friendly, such as mousse, the ubiquitous 1980s hair gel and, most evocatively, Crazy Colour. This new product worked best on bleached hair and was a major breakthrough for street culture and the desire to shock, as before the 1970s bright colours could only be achieved by the use of impermanent vegetable dyes. The punk look mutated in the 1980s with the Goth subculture. Here a unisex look of extreme backcombed dyed black hair with coloured flashes was popular amongst groups of adolescents who listened to music put out on independent record labels by groups such as the Jesus and Mary Chain and the Cure, and the hair-styles were seen to their most dramatic effect in the styles of the New Romantics and pop stars such as Toyah, Grace Jones and Phil Oakey's long-short mutant wedge cut. Streaked hair had by now become the preserve of jetsetting Eurotrash.

**Post-punk inspired
style for Wella, 1980s**

Grace Jones, 1980s

Siouxie Sioux with the
haircut that inspired
Gothic hair, 1980s
Photography by
Joe Bangay

Hair extensions in the
Ionic of 1984.
Hair by Stacey
Broughton, colour by
Annie Humphreys for
Vidal Sassoon.
Photography by
Robyn Beeche

Extensions by Simon Forbes at Antenna

'Wet look' perm, 1980s

White styles throughout the 1970s owed much to the countercultural styles of black hair from the dreadlock to the 'wet look' perm. In this decade the wearing of locks spoke of black pride as much as the Afro did in the late 1960s. The origins of the look were within the tenets of Rastafarianism, which began in Jamaica in the 1930s when Haile Selassie became the self-styled Emperor of Ethiopia who would lead his believers into a black paradise of Zion. These ideas were brought to Britain with the waves of post-war immigration and by the 1970s were eagerly embraced by a new generation of black youth who could find nothing which spoke of their urban experiences in a racist white world. A belief in Selassie

'Afro' plaits, 1980s

**Bobtail extensions by
Simon Forbes at
Antenna**

or Ras Tafari began to be expressed in the wearing of knitted 'tams' in the red, gold and green of the Ethiopian flag, and for women traditional African head-dresses under which were grown dreadlocks which were regarded as an appropriately 'authentic' natural hair-style. This look was further popularized and disseminated by the mainstream success of reggae stars like Bob Marley and the Wailers, whose music crossed into white culture.

Dreadlocks marked another cultural shift from the dominance of white beauty standards but once again the style was incorporated into white culture in the early 1980s with the experiments with hair extensions at Antenna. This process was led by Simon Forbes, who invented extensions in response to demands from white youth who wanted dreadlocks, and was dubbed the New Dickensian look and worn by pop stars of the time like Marilyn and Kate of Hayzee Fantayzee. In this technique molten candle wax was dripped onto false hairpieces which were then entwined with the wearer's natural hair, the process reversed only by cutting it all off.

Olympics Collection at Vidal Sassoon, 1984. Hair by Thomas Principle. Photographed by Roger Eaton

Rastafarian dreadlocks Photography by Alex Marsden

**Almighty Dread,
Brixton, 1999
Photography by
Alex Marsden**

The concept of big hair remained a stronghold for working-class women, resurfacing in the 1980s with the popularity of American soap operas such as *Dallas* and *Dynasty*. The fantasy lifestyle of the wealthy American was adopted through a modified form of hair-styling in the high street where the hair was carefully tinted and layered to flow copiously yet stay off the face. Women began to tint, layer

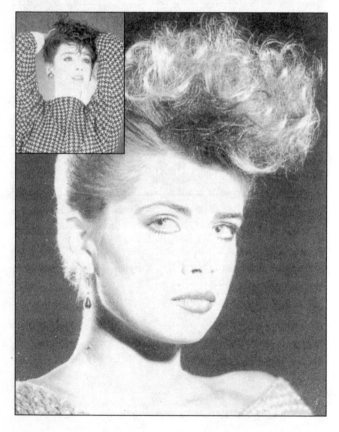

L: Permed hair set with gel, 1980s, Steve Buckle Salon

R: Dallas-inspired 'big hair', 1980s, Steve Buckle Salon

Permed 'big hair' styles of the 1980s

and backcomb their locks to sport a style colloquially referred to as 'big hair', which reflected their version of this image. This helmet of hair as a signifier of female power, wealth and success was best seen in a modified form in the 1980s with the look of Margaret Thatcher. With her rise to power came changes of image and appearance from the traditional Tory middle-class suburban wife, complete with hat and well-scrubbed neat appearance, to the power dresser of the 1980s. To wear hats and to have a set in the 1960s, when she first began to achieve public recognition, and to talk in the genteel voice she favoured were flying in the face of mainstream fashion. In the midst of the supposed 'classless' society of the 'swinging sixties', where to have a relaxed attitude and regional accent was to be in vogue, Margaret Thatcher showed her allegiance to the attitudes and look of her class by her espousal of the shampoo-and-set style. It signified above all a certain kind of suburban respectability, a look which had a lot in common with that of the Queen, a kind of anti-fashion mode of hair-styling used as a way of signalling the unassailability of the monarchy, its resistance to change and its longevity and tradition. A minor change in the hair of royalty is allowable, as long as it concerns one of the younger members of the royal family and does not stray too far from the rather orthodox idea of glamour more readily associated with Princess Diana. However, such a change in the Queen is not allowed. Her fixed appearance makes her subjects feel secure and represents the immutability and longevity of the monarch, who sets herself outside the parameters of fashion.

On gaining power, first as leader of the Conservative Party and then as Prime Minster, Mrs Thatcher began a complete overhaul and transformation of her image. She wore suits with heavily padded shoulders, a feminized tie in the guise of the pussycat bow, high heels, discreet jewellery and, most significantly, bouffant hair. Although hair, particularly an abundance of hair, has traditional associations with femininity and although the late 1950s backcombed bouffant style she favoured signified a particular brand of domesticated femininity, Mrs Thatcher's hair broke the rules. The large, heavily set and sprayed style gave the illusion of a hard helmet and steadfastly situated her within culture rather than nature. This 'bigness' of hair on men in particular has traditional associations with power and has existed as a status symbol for centuries – the hair of Louis XIV is a good example – and it seems the more important the public office a woman held in the 1980s the more 'important' the hair became in taking up of space around the body. In the 1990s the Countess of Dartmouth, Raine Spencer, had an interesting example of a 1960s bouffant, indicating leisure and wealth and a great responsibility to its upkeep as a museum piece. Highly artificial, heavily set hair-styles such as these were a statement of volume and had to be constructed by a retinue of stylists; they needed a lot of attention and grooming from persons other than the owner and consequently provided a comment on the owner's status.

Ironically this retrospective style was in existence at the same time as a revival of the bob as part of the dress-for-success or power-dressing movement in women's clothing. In the 1980s there was a rise in the numbers of women entering the workforce, some in positions of executive power. Countless articles began to appear on the subject of the appropriate appearance for the woman at work, eventually dubbed power dressing. Power dressers wore sharp, tailored suits with padded shoulders, crisp shirts and court shoes, creating a sharp, bulkier silhouette. As one journalist commented, 'The business suit that had been outlawed for years as uncool has made a spectacular comeback ...' Power dressing, a strict combination of short, sharp skirts, shoulder pads and ruthless haircuts, has become *de rigueur* for the

Classic power bob, 1980s

working woman.' This was a form of dress, which was supposed to signify equality in the workplace. The idea of 'dressing for success' was initiated by John Molloy, who advised women to dress 'seriously', that is, in a non-feminine way, for work. He believed that women should wear blazers and tweeds of the colours grey, medium-range blue, beige, deep maroon and rust. They should avoid pastels, particularly pink and pale yellow, to cut out any feminine references and should not wear bright shades, as the wearer would be considered too exotic. At the same time as avoiding too much femininity, direct references to a masculine silhouette were made with the adoption of the shoulder pad. This look signified discipline and control in the world of work; it was some kind of proof that executive women were to be taken seriously and thus had important connotations of

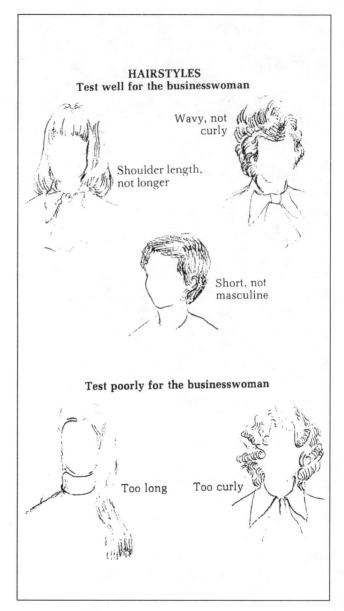

Hair-styles that 'test well for the businesswoman': John T. Molloy's advice in WOMEN: DRESS FOR SUCCESS, 1980 Courtesy W. Foulsham & Co. Ltd

Permed hair, 1980s

gender, power and sexuality. The power bob had to tread a thin line between being not too long, as this would be considered too feminine and therefore frivolous, and not too short as this was too butch. Consequently Molloy was very specific when it came to hair, saying, 'If you are a businesswoman your hair must be medium length. It can never be so short or styled in such a way that it would look mannish or boyish. Women with very long hair can be very feminine, very sexy, very appealing – and non-authoritative. You hair must not be excessively curly or wavy. Too many curls and waves will hurt you in business. If a woman wants to be authoritative she must have hair in the medium range.'[1] Absoloute no-nos in the business arena according to Molloy were dyed blonde hair-dos: blondes might have more fun but brunettes had more power in the workplace and tipping, streaking and frosting were 'unsexy and tasteless'. The power bob began to rule – the right hair uniform for the woman who was going places.

But some found his rigid ideas untenable: 'A woman executive should wear skirts, not pants, and maintain a tailored look with a well-cut blouse, but should always wear her hair short or pinned back. Why? Who are these people to make such a decision? Where are the rules that say an executive is smarter with shorter hair? Is a stockbroker, a doctor, a physicist, or a pilot better or smarter at her job because her hair is shorter?'[2] However, the hair market responded to this new executive woman with her lifestyle dominated by work and no time for play. After a hard work-out in the gym, a woman now no longer needed to linger over her beauty preparations, she could just use a new product like Vidal Sassoon's Wash 'n' Go, a two-in-one shampoo and conditioner. Slowly, though, another look began to break through which was to dominate women's hair-styling until the mid-1990s: the long, tousled perm which in the 1980s was popularized by the Australian singer and soap opera star Kylie Minogue.' Disorder took over from the ordered executive chic which was dominating hair design and

[1] John T. Molloy, WOMEN: DRESS FOR SUCCESS (London, W. Foulsham and Co. Ltd, 1980), p. 83

[2] Wyse, p.171

Permed style with mousse, 1980s

thousands of women bought into the look and continued to do so throughout most of the 1990s. The link between a full head of curls, however they were produced, and femininity was still a strong one and products entered the market to make this fantasy possible. The tight perm, lasting up to three months, had been associated with pensioners whose

Kylie Minogue, 1980s

attitudes to haircare were still steeped in the orthodoxy of the 1940s and 1950s. In the early 1980s young women rediscovered the perm, but instead of having it to add volume and as a prelude to a set they left it in its chemically enhanced kinky state or even exaggerated it with mousse. Women with natural curls received backhanded compliments like, 'I love your hair. Is it a perm?' and the tousled look became a standard hair-style right into the 1990s with perming techniques used as the gateway to big hair. The look was seen to its biggest effect on television screens with the import of American chat shows or what became known as Zoo TV. In the audiences, listening raptly to the tales of woe on Oprah Winfrey, Ricki Lake or Jerry Springer, were mall chicks with Mulleted partners, gals with big, blonde, permed hair and backcombed fringes. This look become so widespread amongst the working-class women of America that its codes were debated at the highest levels. In 1998 Paula Jones, a young woman from Arkansas who was attempting to implicate President Clinton in a sex scandal, had to undergo a major hair overhaul. At the deposition, where Clinton was forced to appear to answer his accuser for the first time, Jones arrived smiling broadly for the cameras, causing the journalist to gasp at her transformation from 'big-haired floozy', one term used to describe her when she filed suit against the President in 1994, to a 'respectably elegant Washington power-dame'. Aware that her 'trailer-trash' looks might count against her in the eyes of the jury, she was put in the hands of hair-stylist Daniel DiCrisco of Los Angeles, who was responsible for the blonde mane of Pamela Anderson and countless *Playboy* cover girls. Interviewed by the *Washington Post*, DiCrisco said he had spent five months

**Paula Jones before and
after the overhaul,
1998
Courtesy Associated
Press**

[1] John Carlin, 'Clinton faces sex – life grilling,' INDEPENDENT ON SUNDAY, 18 January 1998, p. 3

overhauling Jones's frizzy permed look to achieve her softer, sleekly layered effect. 'I removed the perm,' Mr DiCrisco said. 'It had to be taken out. It just wasn't pretty.'[1]

Men were also prepared to venture into the feminine territory of the perm in the 1980s, heralded by the use in black culture of the gheri curl. Hairdressers had been trying to persuade men of the perm's beneficial effects since the 1960s to no real effect. *Hair and Beauty*'s writer Peter Hickman spoke of the problems of recommending a perm to a gentleman having his hair cut. It was 'guaranteed to bring a response varying from shocked embarrassment to guffaws of laughter. A great pity, because with a little imagination, a perm can solve many problems.' Thus a perm was seen as a useful way of controlling wayward hair rather than producing

(L) Martin Shaw and (R) Kevin Keegan sporting 1970s curly perms

a full head of tousled curls. Not many took up his offer though and it was up to Kevin Keegan to herald the way in the 1970s. Helped by the traditional hard masculinity of his profession as footballer, a sporting arena where men can cry

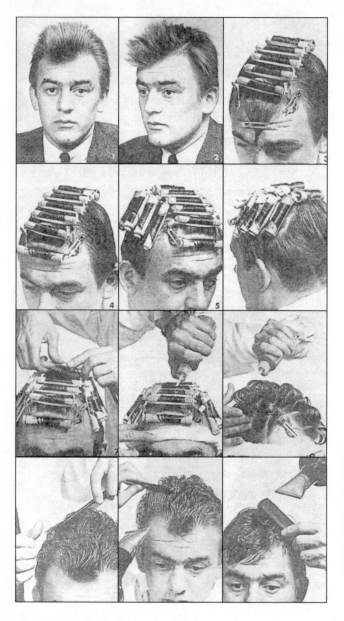

Perming to control 'difficult' hair for men, early 1960s

Finished result after perming

when they lose and not appear wanting, the perm became a new style for the trendy, sensitive yet macho guy about wine bar.

The legacy of punk continued to have its effects and oppositional looks were popular in the late 1980s – there was no real dividing line between where hair should and shouldn't be. The short blonde crop became a cliché, particularly when worn by women, but the real reactions to the 1980s power dressers were the grunge and New Age Traveller movements in the early 1990s. The conservative policies of Reaganomics and Thatcherism spawned a backlash amongst the nation's youth, which had as part of its strategy specific attitudes to hair. Kurt Cobain's unstyled grungy look of the early 1990s was part of a widespread response in both Britain and America to the politics of the right, which seemed unassailable under the leadership of Margaret Thatcher and Ronald Reagan. The look of the stereotypical Yuppie with his short, gelled slickness or the hard metropolitan chic expressed in the bob was avoided in favour of a more downbeat style, a kind of identification with the less fortunate which had previously been the preserve of the hippie and a washed-out look was favoured, the hair bleached blonde as a prelude to the application of the weakest of colours, particularly a gunky green. One of the hair-styles which caused the most public unease was the white dreadlock, which had special significance when worn by the festival-goer or road protester. In the early 1990s a new subcultural group had adopted the dreadlocked look in a matted, 'natural'-looking form, instead of the artificial extensions of the 1980s. Bizarre attempts were made to make white hair conform to this style to signify an allegiance with

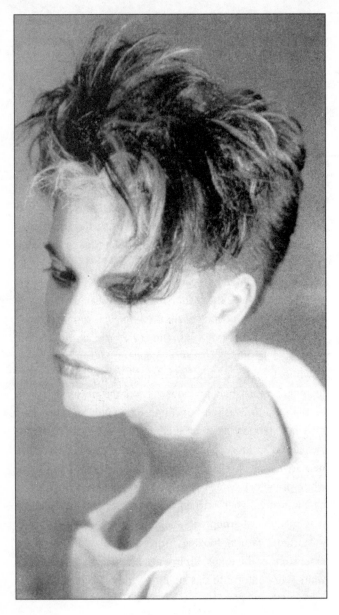

**Post-punk-inspired
looks, 1980s**

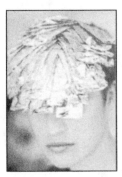

nature and a care for the environment which were deliberately not extended to the upkeep of hair or clothing, and a pot pourri of looks were incorporated into one of protest. New Age Travellers, a disparate group of ex-hippies, punks, squatters and festival-goers, forged an alliance against the Conservative Government's transport programme, travelling around Britain noisily demonstrating against the building of new road networks and attempting to

Musician, Portobello Green, photography by Alex Marsden, 1999

save nature by direct action. The media-friendly figure of Swampy, who had been discovered in a tunnel hiding from baliffs attempting to eject him from one scene of protest, illustrated the typical style of the subgroup. Ethnic type clothing gave a symbolic nod in the direction of non-Western cultures whose habitat and lifestyle had suffered from the same kind of capitalist-induced damage, as did a symbolic refusal to use any kind of hair product which could cause damage to the environment. White youth created matted dreadlocks by deliberate mismanagement ornamented with beads and bells in an almost William Morris-inspired nostalgia for a completely invented medieval past when things were rosy. This rejection of consumerism and an espousal of a back-to-Nature, New Age consciousness diffused into mainstream culture with the Green or New Age movement by signifying an attitude of responsibility to the environment. One of the most popular notions of those connected with this group was that if you don't wash your hair for six weeks it starts to clean itself. Accordingly, the 1990s became the era of protest exemplified by the media's take-up of Swampy and Spider, a New Age traveller appearing as a character on *Coronation Street*. By the end of the decade the traveller had become as much of a media cliché as the punk in the 1970s and manufacturers and advertisers were quick to respond, especially on the back of the 1987 Mintel report *The Green Consumer*. This spelled out in hard statistics that a large proportion of the British public were prepared to buy green products, scared into submission by increasing numbers of doomsday scenarios. Eco-catastrophes such as Chernobyl and Bhopal had struck a chord with a consumerist-obsessed Britain and there was a general optimistic feeling that by taking bottles to the local bottle-bank the consumer could play their part. A magical greenness began to be applied to the selling of household items so that the family purse could be used to help save the world at the supermarket. But biodegradable washing powder, organic produce and non-CFC Mum deoderant as advertised by Toyah were only the beginning. Fashion designers began to display their allegiances to the Gaia principle, some blatantly, like Katherine Hamnett, who caused a furore as far back as 1985 when she attended a reception at 10 Downing Street wearing a T-shirt proclaiming '58% don't want Pershing'. Rifat Ozbek also caught the mood of the time with his 1990 White Collection, which presaged the minimalist aesthetic of the late 1990s. White was the right colour for the New Age 1990s and catwalk photographs of models in white tracksuit tops emblazoned with appropriate slogans like 'Nirvana' appeared in the press. Charlotte Du Cann, writing for *Elle* in 1989, described how 'the green phenomenon has gripped our urban culture like bindweed. Pop music has become world music, thinking has become global awareness, style has become attitude. The word "serious" ("serious money") has been replaced by "deep" (as in "deep green"). TV advertising features landscapes where once it had warehouse districts and cocktail bars and people have been looking back at the sea with mystical admiration. If in the 60s we wished to look like rebels and in the 80s material girls, in the 90s it seems we are destined to appear like born-again Brownies.'[1] Even the American media magnate Ted Turner was prepared to enter into the green fray — describing himself as committed to the cause, he allegedly wooed the movie star Jane Fonda with the proposal

[1] Charlotte du Cann, 'Ever green?', ELLE, Oct. 1989, p. 60

'Together we can save the planet.'

New Age was perhaps a vague and rather all-encompassing term, but it was a very successful way of repositioning products, particularly those targeted at women. One female consumer found in Mysteries, a leading New Age centre in London's Covent Garden, which sold

[1] Linda Grant,
'New Age ninnies',
INDEPENDENT ON SUNDAY,
27 June 1995, p.19

crystals, tarot cards, herbal remedies and other alternative paraphernalia, said disarmingly, 'Coming here is a fix. You can indulge yourself a bit, like at the hairdressers.' ' Caring was the buzzword of the early 1990s and what better word than haircare to enter into the vocabulary of hair products? This, allied with notions of greenness, was a particularly apt concept for the selling of lines such as Organics, with its emphasis on nature, and they were incredibly successful. These mass-produced ranges of haircare products containing technologically advanced ingredients were sold using phrases emphasizing the life-giving, bountiful qualities of nature. The Body Shop was one of the most successful organizations to use the green cause to further its beauty empire and customers were tempted into the stores by being persuaded that frivolity was out of the question – when they bought banana hair putty in plain, refillable bottles, they were actually helping the environment. The hairdresser moved out of the confines of the salon and into the global marketplace, lending his name to lines of hair products and further glamorizing his position as a fashionable figure. Following the success of Sassoon's Wash and Go, well-known hairdressers such as Charles Worthington, Nicky Clarke, Daniel Field and Trevor Sorbie endorsed expensive designer products. These were sold using the cliché of 'big hair' as described by Peter York in his 1995 summary of advertising clichés of the electronic age. He described women's hair treatment ads as 'quite gloriously, spectacularly and uncomplicatedly clichéd in a way that's getting rare elsewhere. The "let down your hair" shot recurs endlessly. Gorgeous thick shiny bouncy hair is let down in Rapunzel slo-mo like bungee ropes. Research-driven director's contracts from haircare companies must specify one such shot per commercial. The research must demonstrate that intelligent women can no more resist this particular image than dogs can resist aniseed. It must, or else why would advertisers expose themselves to universal sniggers?[1] The cliché of the girl shaking her head of wet hair after washing it in a stream and thus producing a 'wet arc' across the frame was created with the classic Timotei girl of the late 1980s. The profile and status of the hairdressing profession had never been higher. A good diet was the key to good health, which was one's own responsibility. You could now eat your way to beautiful hair or take a course of especially directed vitamin tablets.

By the mid-1990s hair-styles entered a period of postmodernist retrospection with heavily textured, early 1970s-inspired looks originally sported by stars such as Rod Stewart and the Glam Rock movement. Crops were in but the meanings were changing. Short hair on men has had many different connotations, but since the nineteenth century it had been associated with the working classes. There were many instances of artists and writers copying this style in a kind of sympathetic identification with poor urban life, such as Emile Zola and Vincent Van Gogh. The Romantics painted themselves without the artifice of wigs to show an authenticity in their work and their experiences — precisely the notion re-established in a more hysterical form by the skinhead movement. The original peanut or skinhead look formed part of a working-class style revolt against the love and peace aesthetic espoused by the hippie and became synonymous with violence on the football terraces and extreme-right-wing movements in the 1970s. The members of the subculture were connoting through their hair the most

[1] Peter York, 'The swimming baby', INDEPENDENT ON SUNDAY, 29 January 1995, p.19

**Skinhead style,
c. 1970s**

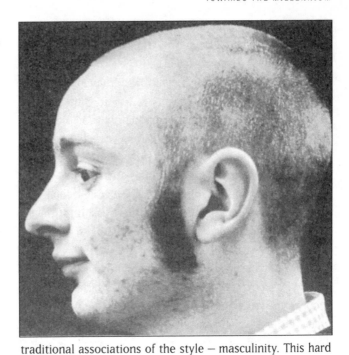

traditional associations of the style – masculinity. This hard proletarian look was followed through in the use of the original worker's boot, Dr Martens, and the violent activities indulged in by the group – particularly 'queer' and 'Paki bashing'. Ironically, a semiotic retaliation occurred in the 1980s and 1990s when the look was cleverly subverted within black culture, signifying a return to the prison connotations of the nineteenth century – it now had outlaw status. Robin D.G Kelly[1] describes the reaction engendered when he as a black man shaved his head:

[1] Robin D.G. Kelly, 'Confessions of a nice negro, or why I shaved my head', in SPEAK MY NAME: HOW DOES IT FEEL TO BE A PROBLEM?, pp.15–17

'It began as an accident involving a pair of electric clippers and sleep deprivation – a bad auto-cut gone awry. With my lowtop fade on the verge of a Sly Stone afro, I was in desperate need of trim. Standing in a well-lighted bathroom, armed with two mirrors, I started trimming. Despite a steady hand and what I've always believed to be a good eye, my hair turned out lopsided. I kept trimming and trimming to correct my error, but as my flat-top sank lower, a yellow patch of scalp began to rise above the surrounding hair. So, bearing in mind role models like Michael Jordan, I decided to take it all off. I didn't think much of it at first, but the new style accomplished what years of evil stares and carefully crafted sartorial statements could not: I began to scare people. The effect was immediate and dramatic. Passing strangers avoided me and smiled less frequently. My close friends went straight to the point: 'Damn. You look scary!'

The gay man had also appropriated this most masculine of hair-styles, converting it into the Nero cut, which by the mid-1990s reigned supreme as the most fashionable style for young men. This look was first associated with Britpop; the sides of the hair were cut short, about an inch long towards the back of the head and the length graduated to the nape of the neck. The key to the look was the fringe, which was cut short and brushed forward, producing a short, cropped effect. This men's hair-style had a long and prestigious lineage stretching as far back as Ancient Rome (hence the name) and bedecked the heads of many famous characters both male and female. In 1883 Oscar Wilde changed from a long aesthetic to short Roman-inspired style having seen a marble bust in the Louvre and Gertrude Stein had caused astonishment with her espousal of the cut in 1920s Paris. Even Roland Barthes, the French structuralist philosopher, had written of the Roman fringe in his seminal work *Mythologies*, where he deconstructed certain aspects of French cultural life. By 1997 the style was even adopted for a

The Nero haircut, mid-1990s

Paul Gascoigne, George Michael and George Clooney

brief period by the Britsh Prime Minister, Tony Blair, and the press could scarcely contain themselves. Blair's brief foray as a Nero wearer was documented in the pages of the *Daily Mail*, which saw a perfect analogy between the look of a Roman emperor and the arrogance of Blair in adopting it. In these articles the name of the haircut was changed with the cultural references improving. Instead of Nero who fiddled whilst Rome burned, the cut was rechristened the Antonius Caesar and Blair's new image change was unveiled at the Lord Mayor's banquet. A journalist saw the banishment of 'the former frizz-prone cut which always seemed to waver between the bouffant and the windswept. In came this shorter, flatter, no-nonsense, decidedly trendier style favoured by the likes of actor George Clooney and Eric Cantona',[1] but this change was not to last, perhaps because the semiotic associations of this particular cut went further: for those in the know, the brushed-forward, short crop had been appropriated through mod into gay culture, ending in the image of pop singer George Michael, and was most ubiquitously associated with lad culture in Britain.

[1] Paul Harris, 'Antonius Caesar', DAILY MAIL, 12 November 1997, p.3

Lad culture, although having always existed amongst young working-class men, was embraced and given its witty edge by *Loaded* magazine under the editorship of James Brown. The lifestyle and habits of the typical British bloke were lauded and became a stereotype that men of all classes responded to. Going to the pub and drinking fifteen pints of beer, discussing football over a vindaloo and then chucking up afterwards had never looked so fashionable, especially when viewed with postmodern irony. Ironic or not, Paul Gascoigne sported a peroxide Nero dressed up with Versace for some of the 1990s. With the rise of all this blokeishness came the re-establishment and trendification of the barber, as a new lad would not be seen dead in a hairdresser's. That was the province of the New Man of the 1980s and he was now regarded as a bit of a wuss, too politically correct and cowed by the demands of feminism. So how did women in the 1990s respond to the lad? Not by emigrating or becoming separatist lesbians — instead the decade was marked by the rise of girl power, which had a major effect on attitudes to fashion, cosmetics and hair. To understand this new attitude to femininity and fashion one must return to the ideological debates surrounding hair and its relationship to appearance within feminist politics of the late 1960s, when hair had never been more at the centre of debate. A reaction against the socially constructed ideas of femininity as exemplified in the dress and appearance of the fashionable woman of the 1950s proved to be a major part of the philosophy of the Women's Movement and had profound effects on attitudes to hair. In 1965 few young women would have batted a false eyelash at reading this piece of wisdom written in a beauty book by the American television star George Hamilton: 'A women is often like a strip of film — obliterated, insignificant — until a man puts the light behind her.'[1] But feminists began to debate the torture many women had undergone to play this part. Susan Brownmiller described a 'time that stretched over many years when I placed myself in permanent bondage to Elizabeth Arden. There, two lunch hours a week, I shampooed and curled with setting lotion, winding papers, plastic rollers and metal clips, gently cushioned around the ears and forehead with cotton wool, tied in a pink hairnet and placed under a hot dryer for thirty-five minutes. Mercifully released, I was unpinned, unwound, brushed out, teased and fluffed into a fair approximation of the season's latest fashion. After

[1] Dahl, p.6

[1] Susan Brownmiller, FEMININITY, (London Paladin, 1986) p.34

a blast of noxious spray I was sent out the door in a forged state of feminine chic that lasted for the rest of the day – that is if it didn't rain.'[1]

This typical 'set' look was seen as symptomatic of thinking of hair as women's crowning glory, the old order of false femininity that needed to be overthrown. The hairdresser in the salon was the enemy, regarded with antipathy and condemnation by radical feminists and by the 1970s fashionable hair-styles were rejected – part and parcel of the social process which constructed the feminine. Fashion was a tool of patriarchy, promoting a controlled, artificial femininity which condemned women to being mere decoration; and the availability of hair-styling and hair products was yet another example of women's subordination, masquerading as personal choice. Feminist writers believed the main problem was that most women didn't realize they were being oppressed when they shopped for their shampoo and conditioner. As Brownmiller argued, 'To care about feminine fashion, and to do it well, is to be obsessively involved in inconsequential details on a serious basis. The desperate wounding absorption in the drive for a perfect appearance – call it feminine vanity – is the ultimate restriction on freedom of mind.'[2] Women, by spending money

[2] Brownmiller, p.56

on a trendy appearance, were exhibiting false consciousness so the new project involved the construction of a correctly 'feminist' appearance emphasizing practicality and utility. Function should come before beauty and adornment; any form of artificial intervention was ignored in favour of authenticity and 'naturalness'. Escaping the constraints of fashion meant the feminist found her natural, authentic self. Germaine Greer in *The Female Eunuch*, a pivotal and popular mainstream feminist text, used hair in her debate: 'I'm sick of the masquerade. I'm sick of pretending eternal youth; I'm sick of weighting my hair with a dead mane, unable to move my neck freely, terrified of rain, of wind, of dancing too vigorously in case I sweat into my lacquered curls.'[1] Hair was on the head but had no other justification than utility; it was not so much styled as 'there'. And it had to be short, Emma Tennant's character in *The Bad Sister* underwent a typical feminist transformation: 'With the scissors I started to hack at my hair. Long pieces of blonde hair, highlighted every three months and slightly curled ... fell onto the rumpled clothes. I almost immediately became calmer and more peaceful. I wandered into the bathroom, and watched my face look out as naked and surprised as a sheep at shearing ... the scissors had reached my fringe and decimated it, little spikes of straw stood on my head ... I could see by looking straight ahead, instead of shaking my fringe to one side, a gesture which over the years, had become apologetic and feminine, as if I had to admit it wasn't my right to contemplate the world.'[2] Above all hair was an essential component of the feminist battle ground, incorporating the personal-is-political ideology to a T – above all, it, like women, should be allowed to do its own thing, be a symbol of liberty, for if it was free, then you were. An early example of the feminist backlash against the artificially constructed hair-styles of the 1960s was the 1968 Freedom Trash Can performance, where demonstrators against the Miss America contest, held in Atlantic City, rejected symbols of femaleness or 'women-garbage' and dumped hair spray, cosmetics and bras in a giant dustbin to expose the male conspiracy that forced women into useless, time-consuming beauty routines. Women were freeing

[1] Greer, p.27

[2] Emma Tennant, THE BAD SISTER, (London, Victor Gollancz, 1978) pp. 49–50

themselves from the constraints of artificial stereotypes as perpetuated by the fashion and beauty industry by shedding their heavy tresses of hair. 'The major proponents would gather an audience together, put a girl with long, beautiful hair on the stage, and then an army of no-nonsense-looking women would come in and one at a time take a whack off her hair as close to the scalp as possible. When the shearing was over, the girl was actually liberated from her hair, it was now lying all over the floor.'[1]

[1] Michael, p.170

The feminist cause was hotly debated in the press, which almost wholeheartedly regarded women in the movement as dungareed dykes armed with machetes, ready to chop off any unsuspecting males genitals, grim man-haters, so ugly it was no wonder that men wouldn't look at them and jealous of any woman who looked better. Patronizing advice was given by male and female beauty writers alike, this one confusedly conflating feminism and hippie counterculture into the same *bête noir*: 'Equal rights are one thing, and I'm all for them, but God created two sexes, male and female, and when identities between them blur, when you can't tell a man from a woman and vice versa, something is very sick in our society. So, fem libbers, fight for what are your rights (and I'm with you), but could you please wage your war wearing an attractive hair-do, a little lipstick, and an outfit that says "I Enjoy Being a Girl."'[2]

[2] Ibid., p.171

However, there were also many problems inherent in the rather moralistic stance of feminism and appearance. The idea of being natural as a woman is loaded with meaning and has its roots in Christian Puritanism. For example, Tertullian, the early Christian theologian, wrote, 'All this wasted pains on arranging your hair — what contribution can this make to your salvation? Why can you not give your hair a rest? One minute you are building it up, the next you are letting it down; raising it one moment, stretching it the next. Some women devote all their energy to forcing their hair to curl, others making it loose and wavy, in a style that may seem natural, but it is not natural at all. You perpetuate extravagances to make a kind of tapestry of your hair, sometimes as a sort of sheath for your head, or a lid over you, like a helmet, sometimes in a platform built up from the back of your neck.'[1] Thus being concerned with hair-styling was evil, a result of the Fall, potentially sensual and worldly. The dislike of feminine appearance forms part of the generally ambivalent feelings of Christianity towards female sexuality; women were seen as a temptation to men. Too much feminine beauty was a trick, dangerously attractive to the male spectator, a weapon in the armoury of women.

[1] Tertullian, DE CULTU FEMINARUM

Feminist dress thus substituted one oppressive system for another which excluded and oppressed non-participants. The rejection of ornamentation in favour of 'sensible hair' became paramount and over the years remained static and lost its political potential. Like other feminist movements before it, namely the suffragettes, it engendered its own stereotype and caused no great changes in the standards of beauty by which women were judged. As Lorraine Gamman and Shelagh Young commented in the 1980s, 'Many women justifiably resent the media for constructing a derisory image of the drab, dungareed dyke. Feminists have participated in the image-making process and must accept some responsibility for forging an association between radical politics and looking a mess.'[2] Conversely it contributed to a feeling of alienation amongst women, particularly younger women who desired to experiment with appearance in a more interesting way. This

[2] Lorraine Gamman and Shelagh Young, 'Radical Chic', SPARE RIB, July 1988, pp.9-11

argument was to resurface on the political agenda in the 1990s. In the early 1980s within feminist theory, the subject of appearance had come to the fore. Some women believed that the frivolity of fashionable appearance needn't automatically subordinate women in the eyes of men. Women who dyed their hair blonde and wore lashings of make-up shouldn't fear being taken for a dumb stereotype. Dressing up wasn't to be confused with dressing for men.

The politics of Girl Power meant a subversion of fashion, to manipulate rather than be manipulated. Fashion could be used as a strategy of resistance. Instead of a repressive system upheld by patriarchy to keep women in their place, it began to be regarded as a form of aesthetic creativity, making possible the invention and exploration of alternatives, an easily available resource which could be used for ideological purposes. This notion had as its antecedents the 'kinderwhore' style of the American grunge star Courtney Love of the band Hole and was duly sanitized for mass consumption in the guise of the Spice Girls. Using hair in particular to make a point about the power of femininity, differing stereotypes were created to appeal to a mass female audience. Young girls chose the type they most wanted to be when they grew up, although Geri's dyed blonde streaks in red hair found their way into a more adult club culture. Baby Spice in particular was very popular amongst the public, an irony considering that the schoolgirl look was roundly condemned whenever it appeared on the fashion catwalks. Young women began wearing their hair in bunches, a style they hadn't sported since the classroom, or in plaits, which had changed from being a look that signified an ordered, tidy girl to something a bit more alternative.

Spice Girls-inspired bunches. Car insurance advertisement, 1998 Courtesy Ecclesiastical Direct

Throughout the 1990s women's styles varied, from the shaven head of counterculture and the festival circuit, as originally displayed by Sinead O'Connor, to the reverse perm of *Friends* star Jennifer Aniston, which consigned curls to the dustbin of fashion. Skinny hair was in and perms belonged to eco-feminists like Anita Roddick of the Body Shop or heroines in soap operas. The journalist Michele Kirsch declared the perm dead in 1996: 'Hair straightening is all the rage. Nothing typecasts a girl quite like a head of curls. In her late teens and twenties she is a new age hippie. In her thirties she is too cerebral to bother. In her 40s and 50s she is an ageing hippie. In her 60s she can go for the Miss Havisham look.'[1] And the magazine *New Woman* had a page devoted to dodgy examples. The look was so outmoded that in a reverse take women blessed with curly hair were going to the hairdresser's to suffer the tortures of straightening serums, hot tongs and even chemical relaxants. It was also in the 1990s that bottle-blondeness began to exemplify a kind of transgressive alternative beauty. Paula Yates, the atypical suicide blonde, was vilified by the media on the breakdown of her marriage to Bob Geldof. In newspaper attacks similar in style and content to those Harlow endured, Yates was reported to be going bald because of her excessive reliance on the bleach bottle. The vulgarity of her hair mirrored her sexuality and she was seen to be suffering the results of both.

[1] Michele Kirsch, 'Let's get it straight, curls are history', INDEPENDENT ON SUNDAY, 27 June, 1993, p. 20

In the last years of the twentieth century the debate still rages around 'correct' black hair-styles. One cultural critic, Kobena Mercer, has debated the whole concept of 'naturalness' and the original black style of the 1960s and 1970s, pointing out that, like any other concept, they have to be created through conscious decision-making and artificial construction — black hair doesn't just naturally grow in Afros or dreadlocks. Particular techniques have had to be devised

Perms from hell,
COURTESY NEW WOMAN
MAGAZINE, 1998

to achieve the 'right' shape, such as the use of the Afro comb, and dreadlocks have to be started off artificially by twisting and curling the hair at the root. The intricacy of the technique can be quite clearly seen in the website 'How to Dread', where the participant is told that they have to be prepared to 'get cozy' as the process of dreadlocking can take about three hours, depending on the length of the hair; shampooing is vetoed for a month afterwards, daily head massage is needed to keep the style looking good and hair from then on needs constant vigilance as the new growth needs twisting and any locks that have unravelled need to be attended to. Despite all this, these styles are regarded as natural and it is a commonly accepted notion that if black kinky hair, and white for that matter, is left to grow long enough, it will mat into strands with washing and oiling being the only upkeep necessary.

Halo cut, natural hair with straightened back, 1980s

This idea of naturalness is a debate that rages in the pages of black beauty magazines. Naomi Campbell in particular is singled out for criticism and condemned for being white-identified because of her abandonment of natural hair for wigs and weaves. She is believed to be exhibiting a form of false consciousness negating the natural beauty of blackness. The male equivalent is Michael Jackson, who appears unhealthily enslaved to Eurocentric notions of beauty, his hair catching alight during the making of a Pepsi commercial seen as due punishment. Notions of an appropriately black appearance seem to place as many restrictions as white models of beauty, and as the third wave of feminism regards the artificiality of femininity as a tool to play with and construct new stereotypes of womanliness, the same can be said for black appearance. Why does there have to be a model, black or white at all? The black beauty model should be deconstructed as well — why should black men and women be limited to a specific range of 'authentic' hair-styles? This would be a loss, seeing as one of the most resonant areas of self-expression within youth culture, both black and white, has been hair, and within the black community the hairdressing and barber's salon has been an important social centre. Significantly it was the focus of the first black sitcom, *Desmonds*.

By the late 1990s hairdressing was being called the new rock and roll; the profession, once one of servitude, had turned into a prestigious business, with household names reaping the benefits. The hairdresser, like the fashion stylist, was seen as one of the pivotal parts of a fashion team in creating new looks for the catwalk. Where now for the hairdresser? The accepted has to become the avant-garde if new looks are to develop. Finding it increasingly difficult to break into the hallowed ranks of the superstar hairdresser, a new generation attempted to introduce the profession to the imagery and ideas of that most fashionable of subjects in pre-millennium times, fine art. In 1998 a newspaper article introduced a 'brazen new breed of barneteers' described as 'doing their best to change hairdressing's traditionally rather luvvie, not to mention camp, reputation'.[1] Johnny Drill, session stylist and subversive, inspired by medical photographs of autopsies and brain operations, displays a deconstructionist approach to the cutting of hair in sync with what is going on in high fashion with high-profile designers such as Alexander McQueen and Andrew Groves. This aesthetic of freakery can be seen at its most successful in the work of the Sensation artists such as Damien Hirst and the Chapman Brothers, whose technique of *épater la bourgeois* is a direct descendant of Duchamp's *Fountain* in the early years of the twentieth century: see Hirst's dismembering of animal carcasses for artistic effect and Drill's ugly-beautiful haircuts. Our particular brand of *fin de siècle* decadence seems to assume that freakishness is the way forward – a rather hysterical response to the dawning of a new age. The salon may become a theme park. In Lee Stafford's, which is dubbed 'The House that Hair Built', clients have their hair cut in a haunted house, complete with cobwebs, chandeliers from the 1920s, and an entrance through a pretend bookcase. Despite all this gimmickry, there are important arenas where art meets technique, such as the work of the creative team at Vidal Sassoon's Advanced Academy. The International Creative Director, Tim Hartley, takes inspiration from the past to create looks for the present using skills honed from years of experience.

[1] James Anderson, Snippers: We're Mad, We Are, INDEPENDENT ON SUNDAY, Real Life Section, 11 March, 1998, p. 3

As ever, hair is the easiest part of the body to alter, as the changes wrought are not permanent. Unlike cosmetic surgery, it's relatively cheap and marginally less stressful, and as we approach a new millennium our attitudes to science and technology, so negative at the start of the 1990s, have changed dramatically. We are caught between a pre-millennium tension, a dystopian view where the world is choked through pollution and over-population, or a Utopian vision based on progress engendered by new technology. As the human body becomes increasingly sophisticated through the use of artificial body parts such as pacemakers and hip replacements, the boundaries are limitless. Artificiality is seen as the way forward, creating new expressions of beauty and, with increasing genetic research, one day we will be able to harvest our clone's organs to replace our own and live for ever. A fear of death underpins Western culture in a post-AIDS world where a large proportion of the population actively believe in the possibility of alien abduction and meteor attack. Youth is paramount and age is decay, so it is up to us to stay looking as consumer culture dictates for as long as possible. Things have turned full circle in the consumer-led society of the late twentieth century. The original stigmas associated with dyed hair, for instance, have completely disappeared. Attitudes have changed so much that nowadays it seems unusual if grey hairs are not dyed — why not if the products are available? — and colourists have become professionals in their own right. These ideas are almost in direct opposition to the immediate post-war years, when beauty writers attributed greying hair to 'the result of devitalized foods and the more severe tension of the world in which we live'.[1] To prevent greyness, men and women were advised to have better living habits but ultimately to give in gracefully and 'make it an asset by the sheer loveliness of its appearance. Many people rave about beautiful grey or white hair when it is well cared for and becomingly arranged. It often lends an unusual air of distinction and flattery to one who would be commonplace if the hair were dyed.'[2] By the 1980s it was taboo to leave hair grey au natural, particularly if one was under sixty. The hairdresser George Michael made this clear: 'The appearance of grey hair, to any extent, should be equivalent to a fire alarm for a burning house — the alarm

[1] Dengel, p.30

[2] Ibid

box is telling you that you need help.'[1] It signified a lack of pride in ones appearance, having let oneself go. By the 1990s the hair, face and body of a woman to be controlled through discipline, diet, exercise and personal hygeine are a woman's prerogative. As she studies herself for signs of decay and is found wanting, she is punished by invisibility. The phrase premature greying is now used to indicate some kind of disease, as if there is an optimum age when greying should occur – part of the philosophy of consumer culture, where to be young is everything. Anti-ageing creams need to be used to prevent wrinkles rather than waiting until the damage is actually done and cosmetic surgery to counteract the ravages of time is perfectly acceptable and debated openly. Even an avowed feminist like Susan Brownmiller is prepared to buy into this ideology: '[I] did not come easily to the decision to colour my hair despite those persuasive Clairol commercials. I thought, and still think, that artificial colour is a shameful concession to all the wrong values. Wasn't it high time, I argued to my mirror and my friends, to put up a fight against the unfair double standard that says some grey at the temples makes a man look wise but makes a woman look like she doesn't care about her appearance? But it wasn't pleasant to bear living witness day after day in all sorts of social encounters to the sorry fact that grey hair does not look youthful, dazzling, feminine, with-it. I hated my martyrdom. I needed to look as good as I could. I wanted to look pretty. Vanity (or was it competitive pragmatism?) won out, with a big assist from a determined friend who came over to the house one Christmas and with lots of teenage giggling poured a bottle of Loving Care on my head. My ambivalence vanished with the first simple one-step application.'[2]

[1] Michael, p.23

[2] Brownmiller, p. 35

Clearly the advantages of consumer culture are too great for women not to participate and a cynicism has developed over the whole concept of green. Science triumphs over nature in the guise of cyber culture and artificiality holds sway. Although the fashion designer Rudi Gernreich predicted that, in time, we would all be bald with a coming together of the sexes in an androgynous future, the opposite seems to be true as our interest in hair remains paramount. Increasingly, wigs are being used in reflecting the postmodern notion of a free-floating identity which can be put on or taken off at will and the transitory nature of what constitutes style in the twenty-first century. The body is now a bio-hybrid, presaged by cosmetic surgery but also by our long lineage of hair technology. For most of the century we have changed its colour and texture through artificial means such as dyeing, perming, bleaching, hair extensions and wigs. There is no longer any such thing as a 'natural' hair-style. But was there ever?

BIBLIOGRAPHY

Anon, *The Habits of Good Society: A Handbook of Etiquette for Ladies and Gentlemen*, London, J. Hogg and Sons, 1859

Antoine, *Antoine by Antoine*, London, W.H. Allen Co. Ltd, 1946

Bennett–England, Rodney, *As Young As You Look: Male Grooming and Rejuvenation*, London, Peter Owen Ltd, 1970

Brownmiller, Susan, *Femininity*, New York, Linden Press/Simon and Schuster, 1984

Cordwell, Miriam and Rudoy, Marion, *Hair Design and Fashion: Principles and Relationships*, New York, Crown Publishers Inc., 1956

Corson, Richard, *Fashions in Hair*, London, Peter Owen Ltd, 1965

Dahl, Arlene, *Always Ask a Man: Arlene Dahl's Key to Femininity*, London, Frederick Miller Ltd, 1965

Darwin, Charles, *The Expression of the Emotions*, London, John Murray, 1872

Dengel, Veronica, *Can I Hold my Beauty?*, London, John Westhouse Publishers Ltd, 1946

Flitman, S.G., *The Craft of Ladies' Hairdressing*, London, Odhams, 1959

Foan, Gilbert, *The Art and Craft of Hairdressing*, London, The New Era Publishing Co. Ltd, 1931

Gilbert, W.S., *The Bab Ballads*, London, Macmillan, 1953

Greer, Germaine, *The Female Eunuch*, London, MacGibbon and Kee, 1970

Gurel, Lois and Beeson, Marianne, eds, *Dimensions of Dress and Adornment: A Book of Readings*, Toronto, Kendall/Hunt Publishers, 1979

Hanckel, A.E., *The Beauty Culture Handbook*, London, Pitman and Sons, 1935

Hardy, Lady Violet, *As It Was*, London, Christopher Johnson, 1958

Kohn, Marek, *Dope Girls: The Birth of the British Drug Underground*, London, Lawrence and Wishart, 1992

Marwick, Arthur, *Beauty in History*, London, Thames and Hudson, 1988

McCracken, Grant, *Big Hair: A Journey into the Transformation of Self*, Toronto, Viking, 1995

Meades, Jonathan, *Peter Knows What Dick Likes*, London, Paladin, 1989

Michael, George and Lindsay, Rue, *George Michael's Secrets for Beautiful Hair*, New York, Doubleday and Co., 1981

Molloy, John T., *Women: Dress for Success*, London, W. Foulsham & Co. Ltd, 1980

Moore, Constance, *The Way to Beauty*, London, Ward, Lock and Co. Ltd, 1955

Page, Betty, *On Fair Vanity*, London, Convoy Publications Ltd, 1954

Raymond, *The Outrageous Autobiography of Teasie Weasie*, London, Wyndham Publications Ltd, 1976

Rees, Grace A., *Reading Character from the Face*, London, Right Way Books, 1901

Sassoon, Vidal, *Sorry I Kept You Waiting, Madam*, London, Cassell and Co. Ltd, 1968

Savill, Agnes, *The Hair and the Scalp: A Clinical Study*, London, Edward Arnold & Co., 1935

Schulman, Irving, *Harlow: An Intimate Biography*, London, Mayflower, 1962

Scott-James, Ann, *In the Mink*, London, Michael Joseph, 1953

Stuart, Andrea, *Showgirls*, London, Jonathan Cape, 1996

Tennant, Emma, *The Bad Sister*, London, Victor Gollancz, 1978

Tertullian, *De Cultu Feminarum*

Trasko, Mary, *A History of Extraordinary Hair: Daring Do's*, Paris, Flammarion, 1994

Villeneuve, de, Justin, *An Affectionate Punch*, London, Sidgwick and Jackson, 1986

Wyse, Lois, *Blonde Beautiful Blonde: How to Look, Live, Work and Think Blonde*, New York, Mary Evans and Co., 1980

York, Peter, *Modern Times: Everybody Wants Everything*, London, Heinemann, 1984

INDEX

A Bout de Souffle 116
Academies 8, 81, 99, 115
Aesthetic hair 29
afro 205-6, 261-2
AIDS 267
Alexandra, Queen 20
Alexandre 93
Anderson, Pamela 159
Aniston, Jennifer 11, 261
Annabel 198
Antenna (see Forbes, Simon)
Antoine de Paris 40,41,43, 47, 67, 81- 95, 142,
    151, 183
Arden, Elizabeth 254
Armatrading, Joan 204

Bad Sister, The 256
Bauhaus, The 121-3
Bailey, David 118
Baker, Josephine 47
Balenciaga 92
Barbie 162
Bardot, Brigitte 131, 187, 203
Barrett Street Training School 73, 81
Barthes, Roland 252
Bates, Alan 118
Bazar Book of Decorum, The 27
Beastie Boys 213
Beatles 198
Beaton, Cecil 24, 48-50

Beatty, Warren 94, 131
Beauty Culture Handbook, The 54
Beeton, Mrs 64
Bennett-England, Rodney 195
Bernard, André 6
Bernhardt, Sarah 87
big hair 180
Bingle, the 44, 184
Black and White 118
Blackburn, Tony 197
Blair, Tony 253
Blaschke, Frank 99
Blatchford, Robert 72
blonde 4,6,11, 159-164, 210, 216-9, 243, 261
Bob, the 7, 51-7, 151, 231-5
Body Shop, The 249, 261
Bolton, Michael 214
Boom Line, The 111
Boots (the chemist) 170
Bosdari, Countess 97
Bottomley, Horatio 71
Boudu 140
bouffant 183-7, 231
Bow, Clara 158-9
Bowie, David 212
Bragg, Melvyn 1
Bressant clipper 28,196
Britpop 252
Broughton, Stacey 223
Brown, James 253

Brown, R.W 4
Brownmiller, Susan 254-5, 268
Brut hairspray 217
Brylcreem 118
Buckle, Steve 228
Burke, Billy 16-7

Caesar, Antonius 253
Café de Paris 111
Calloux, Maitre 82
Camillo, Silvio 189
Campbell, Naomi 264
Cantona, Eric 253
carbon tetrachloride 34
Cardin, Pierre 126
Carita, Maria and Rosy 116
Carmen rollers 206
de Casati, Marquise 87
Castle, Irene 52
Champagne Bubble cut 111
Champagne, Monsieur 9, 66
Chanel, Coco 92, 210
Chapman Brothers, The 265
Charles of the Ritz 131
Charles I, King 15
Charlie's Angels 217
Chelsea Arts Ball 97
Cherub, the 152
City and Guilds 80
City of London Guild of Hairdressers 71
Clairol 6, 165, 211, 219, 248, 268
Clarke, Nicky 249
Clinton, President 240
Clooney, George 252-3
Cobain, Kurt 243
Cocteau, Jean 88

Coddington, Grace 120
Cohen, 'Professor' 119
Competitions 99-111
Coronation Street 167, 246
Countess 171
Courrèges, André 126
Courtney, Tom 118
Cox, Michael 182
Craze, Gary 195
Crazy Colour 219
Cringle, the 152
Culpepers 202
Cummings, Constance 112
Cure, The 220
Curtis, Tony 117-8

Dahl, Arlene 193
Dallas 228
dandruff 173
Darwin, Charles 5
Davies, Nigel 95
Davis, Angela 205
Decoux 82
Dengel, Veronica 172
Desmond's 264
Diamond, Michael 213
Diana, Princess of Wales 5, 230
DiCrisco, Daniel 240
Dior 92, 120
Donovan, Terence 120
Dorchester Hotel, The 111, 167
Douglas, Martin 117
Dread, Almighty 227
dreadlock 224-7, 243, 262
dressed hair 8,18,20-4, 64
Drill, Johnny 265

Du Cann, Charlotte 247
Du Maurier, Daphne 126
Duchamp, Marcel 265
Duncan, Sylvia 116
Dutch cut 38
dyes 154-8, 165-6, 211-2, 267-8
Dyer, Richard 159
Dynasty 228
Dynel 192

Ebony 203
Elizabeth II, Queen 230
Ellis, Havelock 51
Ellis, Ruth 216
Eton Crop, the 44, 49-51
Eugenie, Empress 65
Evansky, Rose 9, 117-9
extensions 223-6

Farrow, Mia 127, 130
Fawcett-Majors, Farrah 217
Fellowes, Daisy 88
Fellowship of Hair Artists of
Great Britain, The 99
feminism 254-9
Field, Daniel 249
Fiorucci 214
Five Point Cut 121
Foan, Gilbert 35, 38, 51, 56-61, 56-57, 75-81,
    147, 156, 158, 176, 210
Fonda, Jane 247
Forbes, Simon 225-6
Friends 261
French, Freddie 93, 112-6, 119, 125
French of London 170
Furness, Lady 97

Gala 183
Galvin, Daniel 189
Gamman, Lorraine 258
Garbo, Greta 192
Garland, Ailsa 120
Gascoigne, Paul 252
Geldof, Bob 261
Gerard, Austin 185
Gernreich, Rudi 126-8, 269
Gillette 29, 59
Ginsberg, Honourable Stanislawowa 82
Girl Power 259
Goddard, Paulette 97
Goth 220-2
Goya 183
Grable, Betty 167
Graham, Billy 131
Grand Royal 213
Grateau, Marcel 135-141
Grecian 2000 211
Greek Goddess cut, The (see Sassoon, Vidal)
Green Consumer, The 246
Greer, Germaine 199, 202, 246, 255-6
Groves, Andrew 265
Guillaume 92

Habits of Good Society, The 29
Hading, Jane 139
Haile Selassie 224
Hair 200
Hairdressers' Guild 66
Hairdressers' Weekly Journal 26-7, 33-4, 36,
    64-70, 72-5, 140-2, 144, 155, 206
Hairdressers' Publicity Group 198
Hairdressers Registration Council 81
Hair and Beauty 193, 198, 241

Hall, Radclyffe 51
Hamilton, George 254
Hamnett, Katherine 247
Hanckel 141-2, 158
Hardy, Violet Lady 20
hairspray 183
Hari, Mata 87
Harlow, Jean 159-61, 161, 261
Harrods 34
Harry, Debbie 217-8
Hartley, Tim 265
Hartnell, Norman 97
Hayzee Fantayzee 226
Hickman, Peter 241
Hill, Benny 96
Hindley, Myra 216
Hirst, Damien 265
Hitler, Adolf 123
Hole 259
Hopkins, Miriam 111
Hornby, Lesley (see Twiggy)
Horowitz, David 199
Hulme Town Hall, Manchester 99
Humphreys, Annie 223
Huxley, Aldous 44-7

Incorporated Guild of Hairdressers,
    Wigmakers and Perfumers 99

Jackson, Michael 264
Jagger, Mick 196
Jeannie With The Light Brown Hair 112
Jesus and Mary Chain 220
Johnson, Herbert 195
Jones, Grace 220-1
Jones, Paula 238-240

Jordan 217
Jordan, Michael 252

Karen, Denise 195
Keegan, Kevin 241
Kelly, Grace 162
Kelly, Robin DG 180, 251
Kirchnerr, Astrid 199
Kirsch, Michelle 263
Ku Klux Klan 160
Knight's Castile 169
Kwan, Nancy 120

Lad culture 253-4
Lake, Ricki 240
Lake, Veronica 167
Lanchester, Elsa 97
Landau, Arthur 161
Lategan, Barry 189
Lavallière, Eve 40-2
Leeds University 150
Left Bank look 180
Lennox, Lady 139
Léonard 66, 93
Leonard 187-9, 190-2, 197
Lewandowski, Pavel 82
Lewis-Smith, Victor 3
Lichtenfeld, Joseph 66
Lisa Wigs 194
Little Women 27
Loaded 253
London College of Fashion 73
London County Council 73-4
London, Gerard 189
Long, Emile 141
L'Oreal 92,155

Louis XIV 15, 66, 69
Love, Courtney 259
Ludwin, Leonard 195
Lusitania 71

Macdonald Brothers 98, 148
Madonna 15
Magic Hair Straight 179
Mainbocher 92
Marcel 80, 100, 115, 135-143
Marie Antoinette 66
Marilyn 226
Marley, Bob 226
Marten, Dr 251
Martin, Madame 68
Mary, Queen 54
Maurer, William 30
McCracken, Grant 183-5
McQueen, Alexander 265
Meades, Jonathan 7
Medusa 18
Melba 139
Mendl, Lady 88
Menjou, Adolphe 96
Mercer, Kobena 261
Michael, George (hairdresser) 199-202, 267
Michael, George (singer) 252
Miner, Henry C. 183
Mingle, the 44
Minogue, Kylie 235-7
Moffitt, Peggy 126, 128-9
Mohican, the 214, 217
Molloy, John T. 232-5
Molyneux 97
Monroe, Marilyn 162
Montgomery, Field-Marshall Viscount 197

Moore, Constance 168, 172
Morris, Edward 6
Morris, William 246
Mullet, the 212-4, 240
Mum deodorant 247

Nero, the 252-3
Nessler, Karl Ludwig (see *Nestlés)*
Nestlés 97, 142-8
New Age Travellers 243
New Man 254
New Musical Express 206
New Romantics 220
Novak, Kim 162
Nu Nile 118

Oakey, Phil 220
O'Connor, Sinead 260
Ogden, Hilda 167
Ono, Yoko 206
Orenteich, Norman 32
Organics 249
Osbourne, Garrett and Co. 26
Otero, La Belle 139
Ozbek, Rifat 247

Page, Betty 165-7
Pageboy, the 111
Pagoda Line, the 185, 187
Pascaline, Mademoiselle 33
Paquin 92
perm 10, 142-153, 168, 197, 206, 238, 242
petroleum hair wash 33-4
Philip, Prince 197
pin curls 84-5, 134
Playboy 240

Poiret, Paul 52
Polykoff, Shirley 165
Poodle cut, the 111
Popovics, Dr 31-2
de Pougy, Diane 139
punk 187, 216-22, 243

Quant, Mary 120-1
quiff 117

Rabanne, Paco 126
RADA 118
Rapunzel 17, 249
Rastafarianism 224-6
Raymond 'Mr Teasie Weasie' 9, 93-8, 111-5,
    117, 119, 148, 152, 165
Reagan, Ronald 243
Rebecca 126
Rendlesham, Claire 121-3
René 93, 117
Regent Street Polytechnic 119
Renato 98
Reveille 198
Roddick, Anita (see Body Shop)
Rohe, van der, Mies 123
Rosemary's Baby 130

Saks Fifth Avenue 87
Sartory, Patricia 181
Sartory, Peter 148,150
Sassoon, Vidal 6, 9, 11,67, 81, 100, 115, 117,
    121-31, 163-4, 186-7, 195, 200, 214, 235, 265
Savill, Agnes 54, 152
Schueller, Eugene 155
Schulman, Irving 159
Scott-James, Anne 95

Seberg, Jean 116
Serventi Salons 194
Sex (the shop) 217
Shaw, Martin 241
Sheridan, Anne 119
shampoo 170-172
sets 174, 178, 197
Shingle, the 44, 46, 54
Sigue Sigue Sputnik 214-5
Silvikrin 171
Simpson, Wallis 88
Siouxsie Sioux 222
skinhead 250-1
skinny hair 261-262
Smart, Billy 111
Société du Progrès de la Coiffure 97
Sol Saponis Aethereal 56
Sorbie, Trevor 214, 216, 249
Soufflé the 187-9
Speakman, Professor 150
Spencer, Raine 231
Spice Girls, The 259
Spiers, Alan 117
Springer, Jerry 240
Stafford, Lee 265
Stein, Gertrude 252
Steiner 117
Stewart, Rod 250
Stone, Sly 251
straightening 179-80
streaking 210-12
Stringfellow, Peter 214
Studio 54 211
sufragettes 70
Superma 150
Sun In 211

Suter, Eugene 148
Swampy 246
Swanson, Mrs 69-71
Sweeney Todd's 195

Tailor and Cutter 202
Talmadge, Norma 45
Teda 179
Tennant, Emma 256
Tensfeldt, Mr 73
Tertullian 257
Terry, Ellen 17
Thatcher, Margaret 229-30, 243
Thénard 159
Three Smart Girls 112
Timotei 250
Titus cut, the 35-6
Toni-Gillette Company, The 168
Toyah 220, 247
Tugwell, Alfred 66
Turner, Ted 247
Twiggy 95, 131, 189-92, 206

Ungaro 126
unisex 195
Urchin cut, the 180

Valentino, Rudolph 48-50
Van Gogh, Vincent 250
Vasco 97
Versace 253
Viking Line, the 111
de Villeneuve, Justin 95, 131, 189, 206
Vionnet, Madeleine 92,
Vitapoint 171

Wales, Prince of 90
Wash and Go 249
Watson, June 205
Wedge cut, The 214-6
wigs 30-31, 116, 192-4
Wild Affair, The 120
Wilde, Oscar 7, 29, 252
Wilson, Erasmus 17
Winfrey, Oprah 240
Wisdom, Norman 96
Wogan, Terry 3
Wood, Roy 212
Worlds End 195
Worth, Charles Frederick 9, 93
Worthington, Charles 249
Wray, Fay 97
Wyse, Lois 164

Xavier 184,189

Yates, Paula 261
Yellow Submarine 206
York, Peter 214, 249
Young, Shelagh 258
Yvette Home Hair Straightening Kit 179

Zackham, Robert 119
Zola, Emile 250